Dear More
DEAR MOVIES

*Other Books by Peter Malone
published by Coventry Press*

Hearts Burning Within Us
Dear Movies
10 Minutes: Gospel Reflections for Minds and Hearts
Christ-Figures

I once wrote to Peter Malone: 'You have spent at least one third of your waking hours living in the dark!' 'Ahh', said Peter, 'but I have had a bright screen in front of me filled with images of life and humanity'. And this is what he writes about in his letters to movies.

I sometimes come out of a movie theatre deeply moved by what I have watched and often have to ask myself: 'Why was I so moved by this film?'

Peter ties many films to various periods of his own life and personalises his responses to the films. He uses his extraordinary gifts of memory and detail to explore themes that emerge through films: forgiveness, redemption, reparation and so on. Films such as *The Nightingale* and *The Drovers Wife* and other Australian movies evoke the 'need to feel and be (and learn to express) sorrow'. Films like *Six Degrees of Separation* remind us 'when we connect, we touch the hand of God'.

Peter writes letters to movies that show human life in all its richness, beauty, colour, light, darkness and brokenness. If you love movies, this book is for you.

John Mulrooney MSC
former college principal, Downlands, Chevalier, Monivae
former MSC Provincial Superior

Peter Malone's new book *Dear More Dear Movies* continues his informative and inviting letters to the movies he has reviewed over the last half century. With a most convivial writing style, the reader is given a tour of the movie, its cast and plot, as well as illuminating asides and occasional theological reflections. The readability of this anthology never wavers and there is a continual delight in coming across films that may not be in the usual packaging of cinematic reviews.

Peter is catholic in his taste and this enables the reader to be immersed in a number of genres. The reader is assured of a warm and stimulating read and the making of thoughtfully curated 'to watch' lists of films that may have gone under the radar of the times.

Peter has a gift for mediating the film, presenting it to the reader with his own sensibility, whilst also allowing that others come to a film with their own worldview and response. Of particular appeal is Peter's memory of his first seeing a film and what was happening in his life at that time. Providing this personal context adds a dimension of interest and resonance for the Australian reader. His observations about changes in the Church and in society are insightful. The asides, detours and movie trivia are fascinating. Reading this book is like talking to a friend who wants to share their unalloyed enthusiasm for this art form.

Peter writes with a candour, empathy and humour and is not afraid of engaging with other views. He admits to briefly earning the ire of The Gippsland Catholic Women's League! His travelling globally as a film juror and his own priestly work adds another layer of richness to these engaging letters that brightly enlarge on Peter's wonderful life in movies..

Ann Rennie
author, *Sunday Age* Faith column contributor
staff, Genazzano College, Melbourne

SHARING
LETTERS WITH SOME
OF MY FAVOURITE
FILMS

Dear More
DEAR MOVIES

PETER MALONE

COVENTRY
PRESS

Published in Australia by
Coventry Press
33 Scoresby Road
Bayswater VIC 3153

ISBN 9781922589323

Copyright © Peter Malone MSC 2023

All rights reserved. Other than for the purposes and subject to the conditions prescribed under the *Copyright Act*, no part of this publication may be reproduced, stored in a retrieval system, or transmitted in any form or by any means, electronic, mechanical, photocopying, recording or otherwise, without the prior permission of the publisher.

Catalogue-in-Publication entry is available from the National Library of Australia
http://catalogue.nla.gov.au

Cover design by Ian James – www.jgd.com.au
Text design by Coventry Press
Set in EB Garamond

Printed in Australia

Contents

Dear reader 11
The Nightingale 13
Ophelia 15
Gunman's Walk 18
For the Boys 21
Murder Most Foul 23
Quo Vadis 26
The Good Catholic 29
Tootsie 32
Ad Astra 35
Six Degrees of Separation 38
Great Expectations and Oliver Twist 41
Rabbit Proof Fence 44
Raiders of the Lost Ark 47
To Sir with Love 50
Inception 52
Joker 55
The Insult/ L'Insulte 58
Judy and Punch 61
The Report 64
Mrs Lowry and Son 67
I Still See You 70
The Professor and his Beloved Equation 73

Black Narcissus	76
Fargo	79
Monsieur Vincent	81
The Life and Death of Colonel Blimp	84
Se7en	87
A Star is Born	90
Scott of the Antarctic	93
Mary and Max	96
The Good, The Bad, and The Ugly	99
Hereafter	102
La Belle Epoque	105
Sorry We Missed You	108
A Matter of Life and Death	111
Fantasia	115
Winter Light	118
A Score to Settle	121
Curtain: Poirot's Last Case	124
Okoributo / Departures	127
Duel	129
Glory	132
Erin Brockovich	135
Dead Man Walking	138
Les Innocentes	142
It Must be Heaven	145
Incendies	148
Irving Berlin: An American Song	150
All That Jazz	153
The Last Temptation of Christ	155

Witness Protection	158
The Tree of Life	161
Enola Holmes	165
The Devil all the Time	168
Phone Booth	171
Crocodile Dundee	174
Jo-Jo Rabbit	177
The Pawnbroker	180
The Empire Strikes Back	183
Kingdom of Heaven	186
The Rainmaker	190
The Last Full Measure	193
The Name of the Rose	196
Words on Bathroom Walls	199
Nomadland	202
Hope Gap	205
Mosul	207
Mass Appeal	210
Some Like It Hot	213
The Father	215
Path to War, The Second Civil War	217
Shutter Island	220
Remember	223
Worth	225
Hail, Caesar	228
Riders of Justice	231
Free Guy	234
Blue Bayou	237

One Second 240
West Side Story / West Side Story 243
Nowhere Special 245
The Drover's Wife The Legend of Molly Johnson 248
Foul Play 251
Good Luck to you, Leo Grande 254
The Bombardment 257
Maxaibel /The Best of Enemies / Mass 260
Titles in alphabetical order 263

Dear Reader,

We will always have (and cherish) our Dear Movies. And, certainly, more (and more) Dear Movies.

I was delighted when readers of my book told me that they enjoyed it, some reading right through, others dipping into the selection. First and foremost, it was the memories. Yes. I have seen that one. What is he saying about it? That's right! Or, I never thought of that. Reminiscences, refreshing memories, experiencing delight anew.

So, encouraged, I started again. (There are always movie sequels!) Here is a mixture of old and recent, of the popular and the well-known plus some of the 'I've never heard of that one'. I hope the reasons (the justifications) for inclusion are persuasive and make sense. There is a blend of the deadly serious (two from Lebanon, one from Iraq, three on World War II...). There are some nods to favourite comedies, *Some Like It Hot, Foul Play, Tootsie...* Agatha Christie, Conan Doyle and John Grisham do get a look in the emerging market.

Which means that this is a blend of the expected and the idiosyncratic. But, all the time I am expressing appreciation of the films, the content and the craft/art. I am trying to locate the significance of the film for me in my life (back then, way back then, and now). I am trying to explore the impact of each film on me – and how it does this. And inviting you to do the same.

Re-reading the letters also reminded me of those strange times in which they were written: coronavirus, Covid-19, the lockdowns of 2020 and 2021. (And who can remember 2020 in any exact detail now?)

I hope you enjoy this selection, reading right through in the order in which I wrote them or dipping in wherever, whatever attracts your attention. I hope the book encourages users to respond to your own Dear Movies.

Some notes on the contents. There are several Australian films included, from *Crocodile Dundee* to the very serious *The Nightingale* and *The Drover's Wife*, questioning the colonial presence and the persecution and mistreatment of our First Nations peoples. Looking again at the context, I do see some quite unfamiliar titles, films made for HBO in the 1990s and early 2000s, substantial and questioning drama. And, automatically, there are Catholic themes and I noticed some emphasis on priests (*The Good Catholic, Mass Appeal*) and nuns (*Dead Man Walking, Les Innocentes*) and trips back to the past include the heady days of religious spectacle, *Quo Vadis*. I would like to highlight more titles but, instead, an invitation to look more closely at the contents.

I have allowed myself some cheating moments (e.g. four films in the final letter) but they are powerful affirmations of truth, justice and reconciliation.

With pleasure, over to you.

Peter Malone

Dear *The Nightingale*,

It is an extraordinary impact you make. While I had read that some audiences walked out during screenings, I had not anticipated your power. You turned out to be such a dark drama, quite demanding to watch. We need some fortitude – and some humility.

Your title is beguiling, the sweetness of the nightingale and its song. But, you rather invert the tone of the title. The young Irish convict, Claire, does actually sing in the tavern but that is also momentarily beguiling because tragedy is about to strike. Obsessive revenge takes the place of song. And, the setting – Van Diemen's Land in the 19th century – is unrelentingly grim.

What you offer is an invitation to go into the depths of human experience in Australia, an exploration of what Hobbs called 'man's inhumanity to man' and, especially in this drama, more literally man's inhumanity to woman.

Your writer-director, Jennifer Kent, made audiences take note in 2014 with her imaginative horror story, *The Babadook*. I think my expectations were along those lines but with you she goes back into Van Diemen's Land, 1825 – a rather unrelenting visit to a time that few in the film's audience might want to have lived through.

I realise most Australians don't go back, don't want to go back, into the history of the continent from the time of Captain Cook and his declaration that the land belonged to no one, was 'terra nullius' with the judgment that the inhabitants of the land were less than human. There was no knowledge then that the Aboriginal peoples had lived and thrived here for more than 60,000 years. Even when this is acknowledged, we still have a lot to learn.

And this is the context for Claire's story, Claire, somewhat shockingly, being as dismissive of the Aborigines as everyone else

– but, dire circumstances, the brutal vengeful attitude of the exploitative lieutenant wanting to destroy Claire, hardens the young woman in her suffering and she herself becoming more and more obsessed with vengeance. As the lieutenant makes a journey through the bush from the dead-end convict settlement he is in charge of to Launceston, Claire employs a young Aboriginal man, educated in white ways and language, devoted to his people, to country, his symbolic bird being the blackbird. They track the expedition to Launceston, a toll-taking journey, violent episodes along the way.

I have to add that your casting is most effective. Most audiences will not have seen Aisling Franciosi, an Irish-Italian actress, the put-upon convict becoming fierce pursuer of the arrogant lieutenant (played against type by British actor Sam Claflin) and his brutal orderly, Ruse (Damon Herriman). The Aboriginal young man, Billy, is Baykalli Ganambarr. Praise is due; each is completely convincing in their performance.

We are transported (as were the convicts) to a Van Diemen's Land you show with its harsh terrain, heavy growth and undergrowth, high mountains, swollen rivers, the beginnings of roads through the bush. The convict settlement seems unrelentingly harsh. The glimpses of Launceston indicate the beginnings of transition from settlement to what the whitecomers to the land describe as 'civilisation'.

We have to learn – it is an Australian duty – to acknowledge that colonial Australia at the beginning of the 19th century was marked by British superiority, certainly to the Irish but, with unwarranted self-assertion, violently hostile to the black population, few scruples in exercising violence towards the men, sexual exploitation and rape towards the women.

You are the kind of film that asks its local audiences, wherever they have come from – prisoners and settlers in the 19th century, migrants and refugees in the 20th century – to acknowledge that our origins have been truly violent, a heritage of massacre, exploitation. And, as we watch this film in the 21st century, we remember that there can be change, with acknowledgment, repentance, an inherited need for honesty and atonement.

Dear *Ophelia*,

Ophelia. No further identification necessary (just as with those other Shakespearean leading ladies, Desdemona, Portia, Cordelia...).

At once, I thought of Hamlet. But, of course, I should not have. As Ophelia's voiceover and insistence at the end definitely remind us that this is her story. Of course, Hamlet does appear (shown as very active, too busy to be soliloquising). While we have heard her story and think that we know all that went on in Elsinore, in fact we have not heard all her story and this is her opportunity to tell it. And, of course, I was wondering why Shakespeare seems to have missed out on important details and characters – and wondering how he might respond now if there is a multiplex in heaven.

I was very taken with your very stylish re-creation of those events, costumes and decor, the castle on a rock, interiors, domestic life, pageantry – and venturing out into the countryside, the mysterious cave of a witch, the pool in which Ophelia herself floats with the flowers (but not as the play suggests). The film is intriguing to look at and the score to listen to.

I had never thought of Ophelia as a little girl, servant family in the court, looking at the boy Hamlet from afar as he goes away for his studies. Ophelia is rather more forthright than I expected, even at this young age, making comments to the court out loud – but capturing Queen Gertrude's attention and growing up as a lady in waiting. Daisy Ridley makes a rather strong and vigorous Ophelia (just as she has been an even more strong and vigorous as Rey when the Force has awakened in female warrior form).

Being patriotic concerning Australian actors, I was impressed by Naomi Watts as a hurt and neglected Gertrude – what we know of her, and even more detail of what we didn't know, the coldness of her husband, the king, tentative attraction to Claudius. And shouldn't some historian have told Shakespeare that it was Gertrude who plunged the sword into Claudius?

I enjoyed your treatment of the familiar events, but, even more, your imaginative variations on the events, glimpses of familiar characters, some new angles on Laertes and Horatio. I particularly liked this Polonius' prose version of the 'to thine own self be true' speech.

But, even better, there are characters that Shakespeare did not seem to know about, especially the witch in her cave with potions, rejected by Claudius, supplying drug relief to Gertrude, visited by Ophelia – who, ultimately, reveals a lot of truth about the past and Claudius' fickle betrayal of her which motivates her to side with Fortinbras and the incoming soldiers to invade the palace. And the deep pathos of the final encounter of the two sisters.

The audience will discover that there are some other details that Shakespeare got wrong! Some of Hamlet's behaviour, his set up of the scene of advice to Ophelia to get thee to a nunnery. One of the strange things – as we watch this story – is that we forget that, while we know all about them from Shakespeare, the characters themselves actually don't know what they are going to do until they make decisions and act – which makes us impute some motivations to them which they haven't quite developed as yet!

It is nice that Ophelia is about twenty, so is Hamlet (and could pass for Olivier's grandson), young, inexperienced, moody, forced into swordplay by Claudius, shocked at the death of his father, forced to kneel before Claudius the King, disappointed with his mother – and organising the players. That play within the play is quite a striking sequence, silhouettes and outlines lit behind a sheet-screen. Hamlet is somewhat ingenuous, romantic, and somewhat bewildered, nicely played by George MacKay. He definitely learns on the job.

I suppose that for audiences who have no knowledge of Shakespeare's play, this would prove an interesting costume drama.

But, for those of us in the know, it is an intriguing sharing with Ophelia of what was happening behind the scenes (and, at the end, some significant borrowing from *Romeo and Juliet*, and why not!) – and Ophelia floating in the water was not the last to be seen of her?

P.S. A word of congratulations to the novelist for her imaginative take on Ophelia.

Dear *Gunman's Walk*,

I had thought I had seen you years ago on television but checked in my files and found that you were not there. Over the years, I've found that many of the small-budget Westerns from the 1950s have stood the test of time better than some of the more spectacular shows of the decade. Those Westerns with actors like Audie Murphy, Randolph Scott, Joel McCrea, are good entertainment, use the conventions of the Western so well, and have some deeper themes. Your star, Van Heflin, also appeared in some fine Westerns like *The Raid* and, the year before you, *3:10 to Yuma*.

In terms of screenplay, you have strong credibility. I have just looked up your writer, Frank S. Nugent, and found that he wrote screenplays for nine films directed by John Ford, including *The Quiet Man* and *The Searchers*. Most of his other screenplays were Westerns – and I was sad to note that he died at the comparatively young age of 57.

I certainly thought of *The Searchers* while watching you. Kathryn Grant was playing a young woman, using the language of the times, a 'half-breed'. She was reminiscent of Natalie Wood in Ford's film, abducted by the Indians, racist-branding by the whites, including John Wayne who went out to bring her back. Those were significant themes for Westerns in the 1950s, especially after such films as *The Devil's Doorway* and, especially the popularity of *Broken Arrow*, James Stewart as the hero but Jeff Chandler is a sympathetic Cochise, changing the stereotypes of Native Americans in the movie imagination.

However, you have a biblical tone about you – a father with two sons, one good, one bad, a touch of Adam with Cain and Abel, Noah with his sons, and the favouritism of fathers like Isaac and Jacob, and the neglect of the other sons.

But, one of the reasons for writing to you is the opinion of Quentin Tarantino. When I found that you were being screened on SBS World Movies channel, I turned on the television. And, there was Tarantino being interviewed by journalist Kim Morgan, seven minutes before you started up and then several minutes halfway through with their comments! The thing is (and this is a phrase that Tarantino uses so often as he pauses midsentence and goes off at a tangent, then digresses with another brainwave tangent) that he nominated you for a series of films which were significant for his *Once Upon a Time in... Hollywood*. He is a fan. [I should mention that the substantial article based on the interviews appeared in the UK cinema magazine, *Sight and Sound*, September 2019, pp. 18-29.]

What was intriguing about the interview was the way he talked about his character, Rick Dalton, as if Rick Dalton was a real actor in Hollywood instead of a character played by Leonardo DiCaprio. The film has all these posters of films that Rick Dalton appeared in. Tarantino explains in the interview how he began his work on the film writing it as a novel. Which means he has an extended, detailed background story for Rick Dalton. After Rick's being a television hero in *Bounty Hunter*, he was on something of a decline and was being hired to play the heavy in films and television episodes (ultimately, like many American actors, finding a successful home in Spaghetti Westerns).

The thing is... (another homage to Tarantino) that Tarantino thought that the older brother in your screenplay, played by Tab Hunter, is a character that would have fitted Rick Dalton perfectly. I'm just trying, once again, to picture Rick Dalton/DiCaprio in the action provided by your screenplay. Tab Hunter in the role actually didn't do too much for me. He was just all bad, baiting his brother (sorry, he actually did want to capture a wild white stallion for him but killed some 'half-breeds' in doing so), sneering at the young teacher, abusive and dismissively racist, and finally confronting his demanding father, trying to draw on him first. I think Rick Dalton/DiCaprio would have brought much more subtlety, more nuances to the role than Tab Hunter did.

I realise now that writing to you gave me the opportunity to reflect on Tarantino and his fantasy excursion into La La Land of 1969, once upon a time, not to mention the brooding atmosphere of the impending murders of Sharon Tate and her friends.

But, let me reassure you, that I would recommend people to watch you as a substantial and significant Western of the 1950s.

Dear *For the Boys*,

I really enjoyed seeing you back in 1991 when you were first released. However, you have one sequence which made a great impact back then, almost 30 years ago, and has stayed in my memory – the visuals, the song, the dance. But I want to come back to that experience later in this letter.

One of the things that struck me is your picture of America at war from 1941 to 1975, with some breathing spaces for different wars during that period. Growing up at the time, some of those periods seemed long, the child's perspective of the slow pace of the years, or steady pace, during the 1940s and the first half of the 1950s but, in retrospect, I am amazed that that is a period of merely 35 years.

I remember stories of entertainers like Bob Hope travelling to entertain the troops during World War II – and I read that Martha Raye thought there were similarities between Bette Midler's Dixie and her own career but that she lost out in the courts when she sued. That was the period of Hollywood canteens and shows in battle terrains. So, once again, almost half a century later, you brought to life that experience of the first half of the 1940s.

Then, almost too soon, there was the war on the Korean peninsula. And I remember seeing Korean war movies in the early part of the 1950s without quite appreciating their toll let alone anticipate the consequences.

While there was something of a decade's gap between Korea and Vietnam, there were many rumbles of war – the 1956 Suez crisis, Cold War confrontations, the Cuban Crisis... But, by 1963, the United States was becoming involved in Vietnam. Your story of Eddie and Dixie and their kind of love/hate relationship, professional jealousies, entertainment relationships developed during those years so that by the time of the Vietnam war, Americans were involved again and, especially, the younger generation, and your focus on Dixie's son, Danny (who, I notice, was played by director Mark Rydell's son, Christopher Rydell).

My impression of entertainers in Vietnam came from those jaunty then alarming sequences in *Apocalypse Now* – the rowdy troops, the gaudy entertainment, the bunny singers and dancers, the always imminent danger. This was in mind as I watched Dixie visiting the troops and her performance. And there was Danny nearby, on guard.

And so, the memorable sequence with Dixie, Bette Midler (who had made such an impression over a decade earlier when she sang, so memorably and delicately, *The Rose*) standing in front of the raucous troops, their heckling, their letting off steam. As only Bette Midler could, she told them to shut up. But, when they were quiet, she sang so beautifully, bringing to gentle life with pathos, the Beatles' song, *In My Life*. John Lennon's lyrics were deeply felt and I felt them most deeply. Gentle, beautiful, and then the wonderful minuet, the tall African-American soldier, stepping out, Dixie taking his hand, quietly dancing, the troops hushed, a perfect moment.

> Though I know I'll never lose affection
> For people and things that went before
> I know I'll often stop and think about them
> In my life I love you more
> In my life I love you more.

Then, of course, for the narrative and your themes – planes suddenly flying over, deafening noise, choking smoke, bombs dropping, Danny rushing to his mother reaching out – and the violent sadness of his death.

I read now that you were a box office failure on release in 1991 and I was disappointed to hear that. But, somebody also mentioned that you had become something of a cult film. For me, you were always a cult film on America at war in the 20th century – but, of course, any mention of you brings to visual life, to the sound of the music and singing, a sequence that has meant quite a bit to me, in my life.

Dear *Murder Most Foul*,

I like the Shakespearean reference, but *Hamlet* you are not. Rather, you are very likeable entertainment, one of those inexpensive supporting features from the early 1960s UK, short running time, black-and-white photography, Ron Goodwin's cheerfully jaunty score, but a good fun mixture of crime and comedy. I think I have written that sentence to you in case anyone is looking over my shoulder and wondering who you are and why the letter. And, by the way, I also really enjoyed your three fellow-features, *Murder She Said*, *Murder at the Gallop*, *Murder Ahoy*. But you won because of that Shakespearean echo.

If anyone were to ask the reasons for writing to you, the answer is easy: Agatha Christie, or, more specifically, Agatha Christie's Miss Marple, or even more precisely, Agatha Christie's Miss Marple in the delightful form of Margaret Rutherford.

I know there have been so many Agatha Christie films and television series (just think of all the David Suchet Poirots). And there were the TV Miss Marples, Joan Hickson if you want her stern and spindly, Geraldine McEwan if you want her softly insinuating, Julia McKenzie in between. And there was, momentarily, Angela Lansbury trying to deal with Elizabeth Taylor and Kim Novak in *The Mirror Crack'd*. But I vote for Margaret Rutherford.

You heard the story that Agatha Christie did not approve of Margaret Rutherford's casting? However, the two women met and became friends, Agatha Christie even dedicating a novel to her, in fact, *The Mirror Crack'd From Side to Side*, 'To Margaret Rutherford, with admiration'.

While I was thinking of Agatha Christie and the mysteries in her own life (remembering Vanessa Redgrave in *Agatha*), I remembered October-November 1956. Those were the months when we were doing our Leaving Certificate exams.

Looking back, I'm rather surprised. We were at boarding school, Chevalier, aged 17, not preparing for, or recovering from, going into Bowral High School to sit the exams but returning to the comfort (or busyness) of being back at school. What I did (and it must've been part of my compulsion to completely complete each task or enterprise) was to read an Agatha Christie mystery every day – which I did. How about Agatha Christie for a revival of spirits or an energising stimulus?

I just had another distraction. Agatha Christie started on an extreme high with her early *The Murder of Roger Ackroyd*, and I was excitedly dumbfounded on the discovery of who did it. I had been perfectly reeled in. Then I discovered a clue to solving her cases (though not always correctly!). There was a most irritating character in *Lord Edgware Dies* (I remembered this wrongly all these years and I don't know which book it was!). I kept wishing he would go away and we could get on with the story. He was a most unwanted distraction, an intrusion and, of course, he done it. And then, *Murder on the Orient Express*, a tour de force.

I'm getting carried away with Agatha Christie and her stories. Back to you and Margaret Rutherford. Margaret Rutherford was already a presence for me, especially her playing off Alistair Sim in the mixed-up schools' comedy, *The Happiest Days of Your Life*. In fact, just a month or so before your release in March 1964, Margaret Rutherford won the Oscar for Best Supporting Actress for 1963 in *The VIPs*. I wonder whether the Academy voters had been watching your *Murder* series – and you would have assured them that they had made the right decision.

I mention the meeting between Agatha Christie and Margaret Rutherford and Agatha Christie's change of attitude. Her mysteries with their ingenuity and teased out by Miss Marple (and that glut of murders in her village of St Mary Mead) wonderfully counterbalancing Poirot and his dapper investigations. But even then, Margaret Rutherford made a difference, large, moving awkwardly at times, shaking on her feet, heavy breathing, sighing, harrumphing, doing something, frequently, which I can only describe as 'wobbling her mouth'. She looked and acted like someone's grand aunt, busy, sometimes fussing, demanding when interrogating, shrewd in picking up clues as certain as Joan Hickson, Geraldine McEwan and Julia McKenzie but capable of being underestimated and, therefore, misleading.

And then there was always Stringer Davis, Mr Stringer, Margaret Rutherford's real-life husband, trailing along or being sent on errands. As an Australian, I like to look back and see our own Bud Tingwell, a friendly but sometimes baffled Inspector Craddock, who was even more successful for decades in films and television when he returned home.

But, as I write, I'm glad I've taken the opportunity, through you, to acknowledge my pleasant debt to Agatha Christie. And, always in the background – and playing in the foreground at this moment – that enticingly jaunty score by Ron Goodwin. And Margaret Rutherford.

Dear *Quo Vadis*,

I think it was you who made me realise that at 11, turning 12, I had a propensity for enjoying historical screen spectacles. In fact, I had seen DeMille's *Samson and Delilah* two years earlier and was quite excited, as well as having a number of Bible history lessons to match the textbooks we had in those days with the stories and sketch illustrations. Here was the real thing, and, forever, Victor Mature and Hedy Lamarr would be Samson and Delilah – and that flashback, of me aghast when a chunk of Dagon's Temple collapsing, fell and drove through the stomach of one of those villainous Philistines.

Oops. It has just come back to me, with the mention of Cecil B DeMille, that in 1950 or so, we had seen his *The Sign of the Cross* in a school classroom, 16mm projection. It is there in my memory, especially with an effete Charles Laughton as Nero and Claudette Colbert bathing in ass's milk as Poppaea. But, it was in black and white, small classroom screen. In 1951, you were much larger than life, 2 ½ hours or more, bright colour, on the screen in the dark at the Regal Theatre at Bondi Junction.

At school, we had been introduced to some of the key elements of church history so this era of the martyrs that you dramatise was somewhat familiar. But, it was exciting to see these early Christians gathering secretly in community, with their memories of Jesus, relying on apostles like Peter whose basic story this is. As I remember, there is Deborah Kerr out in the arena, which looked like the Colosseum, which was not yet built, tied to the post, her dress shimmering in the wind, the crowds in the stands, the anticipation of the lions being let loose from their cages to maul and chew the Christians. (Who could ask for anything more!)

Robert Taylor was the hero and was soon to appear in *Ivanhoe, Knights of the Roundtable, Quentin Durward*, confirming (along with *Prince Valiant*) that I was prone to enjoy these spectacles. And, thank goodness, he was to save Deborah Kerr. A great combination, faith and romance.

The title? That wasn't a difficulty because we had been studying Latin even at primary school for almost 2 years and we knew the story of St Peter escaping from Rome and encountering Jesus who asked Peter where he was going, 'Quo vadis', while Jesus himself said he was going to Rome to be crucified. Potential audiences may have been familiar with the title because of the popularity of the late 19th century novel by Polish Henryk Sienciewicz. As I was saying this, I had a distraction as to how would a Latin title go these days and, suddenly, I realised that I have a preview ticket for next Wednesday night for the space film with Brad Pitt, *Ad Astra*. So Latin, at least in movie titles, is not yet a dead language.

So much of the power of movies is in how they remain in one's mind, especially when a character is embodied in the star. But, for a long time, aided by many of those baroque statues in Roman basilicas, the venerable Scots actor, Finlay Currie, was actually what St Peter must have looked like (and I was not all that convinced by tall and gaunt Michael Rennie in *The Robe*).

While Charles Laughton did make an impression as Nero, he was immediately eclipsed by Peter Ustinov who would continue to be Nero for me for many, many decades. So, that is what it was like to see the Emperor fiddling while Rome was burning, even while, at the same time, he was plotting to blame it on the Christians. In fact, when these times get a re-run in the cinema, from Fellini Satyricon, based on the book by Nero's adviser, Petronius (quite civilised here with Leo Genn) or the huddled Christians discerning whether to stay and be persecuted or to escape from Rome in the faith-based portrait of the elder Paul, *Paul, Apostle of Christ*, my memory returns to *Quo Vadis*.

With my admiration for you, I determined that we would show the film at boarding school, a coup for programming. But, fate or providence was out to thwart me. The screening was forced to be on a day that the students returned from holidays, so a late start, and the very long running time, not congenial really for prime time viewing. The other part of the coup was to have a big poster to put up on the notice board and advertise this extraordinary screening. One of the features of the poster was an imposing portrait of Patricia Laffan as the Empress, Pompeia, reclining in a green dress which was slit up the side of her leg. Father Kelly thought this limb exposure quite unsuitable for the noticeboard – this is 1955 – and so I had to find a green crayon and get to work on un-splitting the Empress's skirt, giving her a respectable green length and not offending or titillating any viewer.

One final thought, a compliment to your impact, mention of the martyrs and lions in the arena brings back your immediate memories rather than the reality of the Colosseum which I passed, going to and coming from theology lectures in Rome for four years!

Dear *The Good Catholic*,

I hadn't heard of you when I first noticed you on Netflix some months ago, watched with increasing interest, took copious notes, intended to watch you again and, as is the unfortunate wont with Netflix, you disappeared (should have Googled). Yesterday, you came up again, so click, a second viewing. I know you won't take it amiss when I say that you are not the greatest film ever made. Rather, you provide a portrait of three priests and a local singer, dramatise their interactions with a lot of dialogue that is very much that of the (21st-century) good Catholic. (I presume that your writer-director, Paul Shoulberg, not only has a strong Catholic background but may well have spent some time in seminary studies, but I'm not sure.)

Audiences beginning to watch you may well turn off rather quickly. You are very specific in your imagery, attention to Catholic details and language. For those not familiar with Catholicism, you are not particularly interesting. The parallel that always come to mind is my beginning to watch a film about Buddhist priests and monks, portrayed with a great attention to monastic and ritual detail which I do not understand, for which I do not have the ability to be acceptingly-sensitive, so a decision not to watch any further.

But, for those who watch, you offer a great deal to consider. If someone has grown up in the traditions of Catholicism and experienced the changes since the 1960s and the Vatican Council, they will be familiar with what has happened in the priesthood, many priests deciding to leave, many re-committing themselves and staying, and many others in dilemmas, day by day, asking how worthwhile their life is, the mundane aspects of the ministry, the loneliness, the need for human support...

So, a fascinating opportunity to watch these priests.

At the centre is Fr Daniel, played by Zachary Spicer. He is not long ordained, does his duty in the parish, has a passion for jogging each morning, was influenced by his working-class father to consider being a priest. (Which reminds me of a piece of advice a psychologist gave me years ago about parents having vocations instead of the sons or, the unrealised pressure on the good son who wants to do the best to please his parents and so decides to study for the priesthood.) Early in the piece, you have a great collage of Daniel involved in each of the sacraments which Catholic audiences would well resonate with. Later, you have Daniel accompanying Ollie, the Franciscan who works in the parish, to hospital and watching how he deals so empathetically with a dying man and his wife.

You have a dramatic opening scene where a young singer, Jane, casually comes into the confessional, tells Daniel that she is dying and asks for advice. Later, she returns. She is what might be called feisty, spur of the moment, whims, suggesting that they change places in the confessional and that he confess to her – not a bad exercise for the priest, come to think of it. But, we discover he has a basic faith, that it is very much regulations-bound, rather cerebral – in fact, he is socially and pastorally gawky in his ingenuous responses.

So, the expected question about celibacy, questioning vocation, discovering human needs that should have been surfacing in seminary years – and, on the evidence of his pastoral manner, the seminary authorities should have been sending him out to meet, mingle, understand himself better and interact with people more maturely.

The other two priests in the rectory are quite a contrast. Danny Glover brings his quiet dignity to the role of Fr Victor, thirty years in the parish, old-style in his way but tolerant, again in his way, of the others. He believes in great attention to detail, talks about a sense of the presence of God and later confesses that because this is the way he functions, he expects everybody else to function in that way. And then there is the Franciscan, Ollie, a wonderfully jaunty performance by John C. McGinley, which seems even better watching you the second time around. He is cheerful, basketball mad, joking, with his choir, especially in a scene when they are rehearsing 'Amazing Grace' and suddenly go into a jazzed up version, he gyratingly exuberant and Victor noting that it is near-blasphemous!

Those commenting on you remarked that the film is open-ended. Daniel goes through his probing of his vocation, especially grilled by Victor who is particularly demanding and rude towards Jane when she is invited to dinner at the rectory. For the audience, Ollie gives a wonderfully sympathetic homily about compassion, human rights, the pastoral nature of priesthood (an ideal sequence for parish discussions). Daniel listens to Victor giving a homily based on John's Gospel and letters, about seeing God, about the nature of love, Victor moving from his rather rigid judgments on these issues to confessing that it is very hard to distinguish one from the other.

Secular audiences who have sat through you will expect Daniel to leave. Catholic audiences, one hopes, listened attentively to the sermons as well as Daniel's reflections and telling Victor that he had come back. But, the drama of your ending is that Daniel goes to Jane's house, hesitates, looks heavenwards, smiles, then removes his clerical collar. Is Daniel actually leaving? Or, given the sequences that have gone before (which many audiences might have listened to patiently but have unwittingly ignored) does it mean that Daniel and Jane will have a lasting friendship while he remains a celibate priest, a relationship that he jokingly referred to earlier as 'a star-crossed platonic G-rated friendship'.

I hope I have done some sort of justice to you – and I would recommend you to Catholic groups to watch and enjoy but also to take the opportunity to reflect on and discuss, in realistic and relevant terms, your issues of contemporary Catholic priesthood.

Dear *Tootsie*,

It's hard to believe that it is thirty-seven years since I first saw you and found you one of the most enjoyable films of 1982. The image of Dorothy Michaels walking down New York streets, Dustin Hoffman perfectly disguised as the television star, hearing Dorothy lay down the law as well as improvising on set, a wonderful impersonation. And, one of the comedy gems that still stays in mind is the scene where the director, Sidney Pollack, playing the agent, backs off from the intrusive actress and, then, his absolute disbelief that she is actually his client, the difficult and temperamental Michael Dorsey.

Foxtel actually programmed you this week in the column of Movie Greats. It seemed the obvious thing to record you and to sit down again and see whether you have the same impact as in 1982 – or, had I changed, since 1982?

Let me tell you this story about *Muriel's Wedding*. The first time I saw it, it seemed hilarious. The second time I saw it, some months later, I mostly noticed how sad, even melancholic, it was. And so it was with you – the memories of all the funny bits, but now something of a bit more sombre tone.

One of the first things I notice this time is how much the #Me Too movement had become part of my consciousness. And you're not the only film that has amazed me – in the sense that there was all that sexual harassment, putdowns, intrusive innuendo and behaviour, blatant sexism all, in a sense, taken for granted that this was how men behave towards women.

It is interesting that your screenplay was written by two top comic writers, Larry Gelbart and Marray Schisgal, and that they have incorporated quite a lot of critique of this sexually aggressive chauvinist behaviour – with allusions to feminist movements. But, in the third decade of the 21st century, we are more sensitive (at least I hope so) in our response to being presented with dramatisations of this behaviour. They have been the subject of many court cases in recent years. While Harvey Weinstein, confident movie producer, has become the symbol of the harassing male, so many other men have been taken to court.

This was not quite the response I had been expecting when I pressed the play button. Yes, while the comedy is still entertaining, especially the sequences of filming the soap opera, and the surprise delight of finding Bill Murray with a substantial role, it is the issues between men and women, taken for granted macho attitudes and behaviour, glib comments about male and female differences, that equality and inequality, that seemed more serious – and they were.

With that, I thought I'd better look up my review at the time – the issues touched on only briefly. I was rather disappointed in acknowledging that that was the way we were back then. But, over the decades, I have written a series of discussion questions for so many films, so I hurriedly looked to see what I had written there. You may be interested to check out what I wrote at the time – and am now somewhat relieved that I wasn't quite insensitive in those days. Here is question 4, rather longer than usual:

> The feminist themes of the film: the background of the women's movement, liberationist movements? The themes of equality? Rights of women and their treatment? The highlighting of male chauvinism, male dominant attitudes being taken for granted? The nature of true equality, in persons, opportunities, respect? The film's use of stereotypes and roles to highlight points? Characteristics of everyday behaviour, attitudes? Experience and learning by experience? The theme of a man experiencing what it is to be a woman? A woman learning independence and equality via the man disguised as woman? The woman being at home with the man disguised as woman? Michael's comment that he was a better man when he was

a woman, etc.? How persuasive the feminist themes? Via character and incident rather than preaching?

You were blessed by having expert writers, an experienced director (who could also act), Dustin Hoffman committing himself to the ambiguities and subtleties of his impersonation career, Oscar-winning Jessica Lange, Dabney Coleman and George Gaines dramatising what it was like to be, even on a small scale, to have the characteristics of the sexual predator – and all in the context of the filming of a soap opera relished by the fans.

By your being included in television sections of Movie Greats, I hope a lot of people tune in and are surprised by how relevant (and sometimes critical) your central issues are.

P.S. Would you believe that during the afternoon of the day I wrote to you, I was asked to respond to three on-line modules for the Heart of Life Centre where I teach, a requirement for all staff members? The modules were: Safeguarding Essentials, Essentials of Harassment and Bullying, Sexual Harassment.

Dear *Ad Astra*,

Before I went to see you, I heard a radio commentator describe you as 'a cerebral Space Odyssey'. I have had a propensity for watching Space Odysseys for over fifty years, having been completely captured and captivated by Stanley Kubrick's masterpiece. I suppose I have always been on the lookout for such odysseys (rather than action shows) from *Solaris*, to *Alien*, to *Gravity*. And, now here you are in that tradition.

One of the major realisations for my life, even from seeing *2001*, was that I had no desire to go into space – except cinematically! And this was a year or more before the 1969 moon landing. One of my dreaded phrases, as I watched the space films, is 'Lost in Space'. The popular tagline, 'in space no one can hear you scream', reminds us that space and our vast universe could swallow us up and no one would know. Which is actually one of your major themes.

(Reflecting on what I just said to you, I realise I'm not particularly adventurous, not a risk-taker in terms of exploration – I cannot imagine my Irish ancestors taking their extraordinarily long and perilous ship voyage to Australia in the 19th century. But, it does occur to me that I'm not averse to long haul flights and being up in the air for so long – but, definitely not in space!)

Kubrick's 20th-century *Space Odyssey* was also a cinema poem on what it is to be human, our simian ancestry, our science and exploration, the mysticism of our future, and the question about transcendence beyond the human, the symbol of the monolith. Then came the moon landing, films about exploration, and the propensity of the human imagination to create horror films.

Watching you, I realise that 21st-century Space Odysseys are taken for granted, that humans go to the moon, aim for Mars, even beyond, and the quest for evidence of intelligence and intelligent life out there amongst the stars. So, your title is very apt. But, there are two ways of interpreting *Ad Astra*, going to the stars (and the Air Force motto) but also looking into the stars, the implications of the vast mysteries in the beyond.

Which means, then, that your hero, an ordinary Everyman of the 21st-century, Roy McBride (with effective casting of Brad Pitt) goes on a journey like Odysseus/Ulysses – and wanders on his return home.

Your setting is the near future which looks rather like much of our present although the transport to the moon seems better than some of our planes and, there on the moon are moon-port, escalators, even a Subways… But, a huge amount of technology has been transported from earth to the moon and to the technology centres on Mars. Your screenplay takes for granted this kind of progress.

But, issues of human destiny, fate, the search for intelligence, become more significant. Roy is expert as an astronaut but he is introverted (moving amongst people but, as he says, always looking for the exit), capable of solitude – and he has a voice-over commenting on this and flashback inserts about his ineffectual relationships.

Then a key theme emerges. Roy goes in search, urged by the government authorities who are suspicious, to find his celebrated astronaut father, sent on the Lima Project to find intelligence, who has disappeared but who may still be out there. And in fact he is, in the form of Tommy Lee Jones. But the key theme is that of hubris, taking oneself more than seriously, usurping authority and power, one's own destiny becoming more important than any of the consequences. Destiny is the word your screenplay uses. There is a mention of fate, but the Greek word that is the consequence of hubris, nemesis, fate catching up with hubris and overpowering it.

By the end, you have offered two contrasting approaches to our future in space exploration. The famed astronaut seeks himself, his reputation and power, is equal to his commission and research.

The Everyman astronaut has to make decisions about these issues, complicated by the father-son relationship and the temptation to emulate his father. But his other option is to retrieve the research information, to return, to reflect on his humanity and destiny without hubris, repairing broken relationships, acknowledging the importance of life and love, to submit... And, like Homer's Odysseus, to return home (yes, home is where the heart is). Home.

Dear *Six Degrees of Separation*,

I really enjoyed watching you, twenty-six or so years ago. And was delighted that you were directed by Fred Schepisi. In fact, I drew on you for an introduction to a collection of short stories. I thought you might be interested to read some of what I wrote back then in the late 1990s.

> It's a tantalising phrase: 'six degrees of separation'. Playwright John Guare has his central character, New York socialite, Ouisa Kittredge, reflect with her daughter about how the lives of every person on the planet are linked. We are only six people away from everyone else. If only we could find the right six. St Paul says something along the same lines in his letter to the Romans, the life and death of each of us has its influence on others.
>
> Rather than at the degrees of separation, I like to look for the degrees of connectedness. We are connected to everyone on the planet, six degrees of interconnection, perhaps. E. M. Forster wisely had this epigraph for *Howard's End*: 'Only Connect'.
>
> Ouisa Kittredge enjoyed chatting and gossip. She and her husband, Flan, are able to dine out on how they were taken in by a hustler pretending to be the son of Sidney Poitier – and who promised them parts as extras in the movie version of *Cats*. As she realised how much this strange encounter had meant to her, she upbraided fellow gossip-guests for making her story merely an anecdote. For her, it was ultimately a profound experience.
>
> Not that anecdotes do not have value. We delight in stories and storytelling. At their best, they capture the experience

but the point about having experiences that they mean something for our lives. (After not enjoying the first part of *Cats* very much, I found myself challenged when the second part used T. S. Eliot's wise caution: 'to have the experience but miss the meaning'.)

Ouisa Kittredge also tells the story of a visit to the Sistine Chapel, as she was taken up on an elevator and one of the restorers of Michelangelo's ceiling invited her to reach up, leap and hit the hand of God giving life to Adam. She does it. She laughs. She is exhilarated. At the end of the film, reflecting on what she had experienced and learned from, and her affection for, her unexpected con-man guest, she walks along the New York Street. She suddenly leaps and reaches up to hit and touch...

When we connect, we touch the hand of God.

Foxtel rightly programmed you recently on Movie Greats. I watched you again, wondering about my reactions, delighted in the wordiness of the screenplay by Guare himself, lots of conversation, lots of art and arts references, lots of gossip. What struck me this time was the snobbery of the Kittredges, the taken-for-granted luxury of the affluent life and lifestyle, chats with friends, turning experiences into anecdotes. It struck me to ask myself whether I was being snobbish, a snobbish looking down on the affluent, their frippery, their frivolous touches, judging them as superficial. And, an embarrassing question for myself, whether I was being snobbish as I enjoyed and recognised practically every art and literary reference. Yes, I did enjoy this. It sounds as if I'm confessing a guilty pleasure.

One of your wonderful features is your musical score, the rhythms, the lilt and lunging of strings in your tango theme – and then the range of piano variations. I don't usually notice a musical score so much, but I'm really enthusiastic about yours. Compliments to Jerry Goldsmith I remember being intrigued at the time about your key plot (actually based on a real character in the 1980s), the hustler claiming to be Sidney Poitier's son. Listening to all the praise of Poitier this time, it also has something like a eulogy of the actor himself. Back in those days, we hardly knew who Will Smith was. While appearing on television and video shorts, this was his second feature film. So now, after so many comedies, dramas, blockbusters and a powerful reputation, we can see how skilled and personable he was at the beginning of his screen career.

In more recent times, there has been a lot of discussion about psychological states, recognition of psychopaths (and a seeming movie and television series preoccupation with serial killers), and recognition of sociopaths. Watching it this time, it seemed to me that Will Smith's character, Paul, was an extraordinary sociopath. He had the sociopath's charm, abundant and overflowing, as well as the complete self-absorption, seeing people only in relation to himself, his needs, his hopes, his joy. This had an extra frisson in the 1990s with his being a gay man, and gay relationships as part of his sociopathic relationships, so much less of an issue twenty-five years later.

While he did delight in entertaining his 'victims', he was still using them, relying on pathos when they found out the truth – but his sociopathic charm was destructive in his seduction of the musician and the musician's killing himself. Paul could be so seductive, seducing his victims but also seducing us, the audience, that we had more pathos for his final confession and going to prison than for the dead man in the street.

I would never want to be part of this kind of New York wealthy chattering class, but you invite a more than willing suspension of disbelief so that we enter into their story, their anecdotes, charmed by Paul. And so, I was very glad that Ouisa went beyond this, upbraiding her husband and friends, and bringing us, your audience, more down-to-earth even as we shared her leap and her reach... to touch the creative hand of God.

Dear *Great Expectations* and *Oliver Twist* (to Dickens through David Lean),

You would realise I'm going back seventy years or more. I'm certain that's true for you, *Great Expectations*, because I remember seeing you when I was small and when we lived at Maroubra Junction. Not sure when I saw you, *Oliver Twist*, but it would have been about that time. Perhaps it was at school – although, as I think back, you have some very frightening sequences with Robert Newton's Bill Sykes, too strong for boarders at a primary school.

Whatever the case, I saw you both before I was ten. I don't know whether most people can project themselves back into their past, remember being young, remember being small, remember what they were thinking or how they were feeling at those times. But, with both of you, I find I can go back into that past, at least for some moments. And, one of the things that strikes me now, is that I remember the earlier parts of you both rather than your later developments, the resolutions, some of the adult stuff!

I had better express my thanks to David Lean for bringing both of you to life so vividly, your powerful black-and-white photography, the condensed storytelling of Dickens' classics, and some memorable performances, especially Alec Guinness, who will always be Fagin for me.

I'm not sure I knew what convicts were when I first saw you, *Great Expectations*, but Finlay Currie's Magwich has always been the archetypal convict. I know he was in many sequences but, you know what I'm going to say: when Pip was quietly there in the cemetery in the fens, the camera looking at the gravestone, and, as I literally jumped out of my seat with shock, fear and uncertainty, there was the threatening, almost-savage Finlay Currie, violently shaking Pip. So it seems that while we might later grow up to be stoic or phlegmatic, we do have our lastingly impressionable moments.

The other long-staying memory of you, certainly not obliterated by other versions, is of Pip going with Estella, with the young Jean Simmons so spoilt, so patronising, so supercilious, yet Pip (and I) charmed and forgiving towards her, to visit Miss Havisham. I can see the cobwebs now, the dark room, spiders and the wedding cake, Martita Hunt sitting there in her once-beautifully-white wedding dress, enthroned in decaying splendour, hear her haughty voice, only later realising how manipulative she was in taunting Pip, seeking some kind of compensation for her jilted isolation and loneliness.

I know there was more to the film – Pip growing up as John Mills, Valerie Hobson with statuesque haughtiness as Estella, and your introducing Alec Guinness as the good, cheerful Herbert Pocket. But, back in the late 40s, that was the adult stuff and, when I had the opportunity at the Australian National University in 1961 to read most of Dickens, your memories were there to bring you to literary life.

I still remember some opening sequences of you, *Oliver Twist*, with Oliver's mother, in dread black-and-white photography, climbing to the workhouse gates, her dying, Oliver being born, first destined to wealth because of family background, but destined to cruel institutional servitude in his early years. And, of course, the hungry Oliver, 'Please, sir, could I have some more?'. I suppose, since my own mother had died only a few years before, so young, aged only thirty, I was empathising with Oliver.

But, of course, what remains in the memory so vividly is Oliver led by The Artful Dodger to that sinister upper room and the introduction to Fagin. And, Fagin for me has always looked like Alec Guinness, sounded like Alec Guinness, looking frighteningly malevolent, often sounding wheedlingly charming, lessons in how to pick a pocket or two, and Oliver, naive, out in the streets, not the most adept pickpocket in London. And I do remember feeling terrified of Bill Sykes, that way that Robert Newton had of looking sinisterly malicious, a touch of eye-rolling, a crackle in his voice –

and now, I'm remembering the pathos of Nancy, her kindness, Bill Sykes's ultimate victim.

Once again, you have a happy ending, Oliver restored. But that did not make quite the powerful impression that the activities in Fagin's room certainly did.

I've since seen many versions of you both, always in colour which seems to lessen somewhat your impact. I have seen a number of Pips, both young and older, some very good actors as Fagin, from George C Scott to Ben Kingsley. But, and here comes a confession, I have enjoyed Lionel Bart's *Oliver*, seen it on stage, enjoyed the film. And, although they are mainly cheery or, at least, sung in a very cheery tone, I do like *Food Glorious Food, Consider yourself, Pick a Pocket or Two, I'm Reviewing the Situation, I'd Do Anything*, and the yearning of *Where is Love*? Perhaps those are the sounds of Oliver. But you, cinema classics, have the images, the Dickensian images, of Pip, Estella and Oliver, and, one can only say the 'Dickensian images' of Magwich, Miss Havisham, Bill Sykes and Fagin.

So, another vote of thanks for David Lean.

Dear *Rabbit Proof Fence*,

I am sure that you remember that Prime Minister, Kevin Rudd, made his apology in Parliament House to and for The Stolen Generations. Which was five years or so after you were released. The Prime Minister at that time, John Howard, was not to approve of the apology – the extent to which he would go was to express, in 1999, regret.

Your story certainly evokes regret. But it powerfully makes us realise that a strong apology was certainly in order.

I have realised that one of the ways of growing in understanding of Australian Aborigines is to look at Aboriginal stories on screen. In 2002, the year of your release, there were several other significant films with Aboriginal themes: Rolf De Heer made *The Tracker*. Paul Goldman *Australian Rules*, Craig Lahif made the drama about the arrest of Max Stuart, accused of murdering a girl, but his cause taken up by, amongst others, Rupert Murdoch in his working for justice days (and the efforts of a former priest in my religious congregation, Tom Dixon, to help with translations from the Arunta language) and indigenous director, Ivan Sen, won awards at the Berlin Film Festival with *Beneath the Clouds*.

You are a story of the Stolen Generation. In 1930, three young girls (two of whom in their 80s, appear in your final scenes to add some heart-rending detail of how their story happened all over again with the next generation) escaped from a settlement presided over by a government official who had 'protective' rights over all Aborigines in Western Australia and returning home in a months' long trek along the fence erected to keep out rabbits.

It was interesting to contrast the colonial culture, forthright in its management of Empire, contrasting with Aboriginal culture, more interior, more focused on tradition, myths and lore. The white culture was action-oriented and governed by bureaucratic detail while the Aboriginal culture was more perceptive, in some ways more live and let live, although Molly, the young leader of the three girls, was quite decisive in her ways.

I would like to reflect with you on the role of Mr Neville. The world of Mr Neville, the official 'Protector' played with earnest righteousness that manifested itself in an unswerving paternalism by Kenneth Branagh, is one of clear (and unquestioned) principles. These 'objective' criteria included such policies as the lighter the skin, the more clever the child, which he alone could authoritatively determine. He quotes mathematical statistics to explain how their Aboriginal blood can be 'bred out of them'. This is the logic of supremacy. Mr Neville (whom the children nickname 'Mr Devil') does appreciate that he does not understand the Aboriginal mind: 'they may have neolithic tools but they do have neolithic minds'. 'The natives must be helped.' Just thinking about these attitudes makes me realise that an apology is essential.

He is outwitted by Molly's combination of doggedness and ingenuity as she takes the children on their epic walk, surviving off the land, making friends along the way and good luck. Mr Neville laments, 'If only they would understand', 'My plans are in jeopardy'.

I would also like to reflect with you on the experience of the young girls, the shock of their being abducted from their desert home, separated from their mothers and their families, from the world in which they live. It is a world of loving relationships that can make no sense of their being taken to the custody of the institution, let alone the minutiae of the rubrics for orderly living there. Their language is referred to by the nurses as 'That jabber'. The only reality for them is HOME. This is the reality expressed in the voiceover comments and in the statements by the two surviving sisters at the end.

Again, thinking of the contrast between the worlds, Mr Neville, his secretary and the home officials live in a world of rules and regulations, of forms, of budget and cost preoccupations.

The externals of Mr Neville's office are neat and tidy. Everything is orderly as the criteria are scrupulously applied. Duty means responsibility. This contrasts with the world of Molly and the girls. Their senses of seeing and hearing are acute. They are able to elude the Aboriginal tracker pursuing them by moving into the water, by disguising their tracks. Their sense of traditional lore helps them to find food, to follow the sun, to work out where the rabbit proof fence might be so that they can follow it home.

The apology to the Stolen Generation issue that dogged Australian society and politics from the early 90s emerges as an echo of the differences between the protectors who knew they were doing the right thing and the people whose lives were often destroyed by the separation of children from parents and families.

You are proof for us Australian late-comers to the land that we need to feel and be (and learn to express): Sorry.

Dear *Raiders of the Lost Ark*,

Thinking about my letters to *Dear More Dear Movies*, I decided to have another look at you because you were certainly exciting, to say the least, back in 1981. But watching you now made me realise that is often very difficult to recapture that spirit of the times, that first fervour, the introduction and first meeting, that enthusiasm. After all, it was almost four decades ago and we have grown older with you, are used to your presence. And, of course, Indiana Jones went off to the Temple of Doom, to the Last Crusade, to the Kingdom of the Crystal Skull (perhaps a bit too late and not so well). He had his own series of tele-movies, *Young Indiana Jones* – and we even discovered that, at one stage, he looked like River Phoenix and that Sean Connery was his father!

Thinking of 1981 reminded me that there were really few action superheroes in those days, not those with superhuman gifts. They were there on the television screen and, especially, in the comic strips and comic books. But our imaginations were in processes of change. Even at the time, I thought there was an extraordinary (cataclysmic/culture-changing) transformation with *Star Wars* emerging in 1977. There was a pre-*Star Wars* era and we are well into a post-*Star Wars* era. And, just ask anyone now sixty years of age and under about their memories – and, as I write, the conclusion to the third trilogy is due for release!

We were invited to go beyond ourselves, into the galaxies, to worlds of myths and mythologies, to suggestions of transcendence with The Force. And, of course, Harrison Ford was there as Han Solo – and again in *The Empire Strikes Back* in 1980. George Lucas himself contributed to your story.

But, the superheroes were making a move to emerge from of the comics, especially DC Comics. 1978 brought us *Superman:*

The Movie, with that most genial of superheroes, kryptonite-resistant Christopher Reeves' Superman. But this meant in 1981 that we weren't quite expecting Indiana Jones and not necessarily anticipating what could be called the Indiana Jones Universe! So, all thanks to Steven Spielberg.

However, there is one way of re-capturing that initial response, what we felt when we were younger, or at least mine: the film review. On re-reading my brief review of the time, I was more than surprised at my zest but rather pleased that there was some record of my enjoyment, a memory of the way we were. So, I don't know whether you remember my review at the time, but I will share it with you now:

> *Raiders of the Lost Ark* hits the jackpot. George Lucas proves again that audiences love a good yarn, the far-fetched adventures of upright heroes, strong heroines, snarling, sadistic villains and cliff-hanging climaxes. They come thick and fast here, blending real suspense (snakes, boulders) with hilarity. Hitler is after the Ark of the Covenant in the mid-'30s but hero, Indiana Jones (played by *Star Wars'* Han Solo - Harrison Ford) prevents him in a replay of serial clichés, presented good-humouredly but straight, that is both hugely entertaining and a nostalgic tribute. Karen Allen is an attractively sturdy heroine. Steven Spielberg keeps it going at a rattling pace – almost defying anyone not to enjoy it.

I am more than a little embarrassed that I did not mention John Williams' score but I enjoyed its main theme and how it kept recurring as Indy continually strode into action. After all, we were definitely ready because John Williams had scored *Star Wars* and *Superman: the Movie* (and *ET* was just around the corner – and I am still moved by his score for *Schindler's List*)

I do have what was, for me, a major complaint. It's in your screenplay. Since I taught Scripture studies for many years (and was doing so when you were released), I was shocked, scandalised and dismayed when we were told that the Ark of the Covenant disappeared in 980 BC. While that may have been convenient for your action, especially since the Ark allegedly disappeared into a mysterious Egyptian city, I just wanted to put in a reminder (and you've probably heard this a number of times from those well acquainted with the Jewish Scriptures) that it is very clear that the Ark of the Covenant actually disappeared when Nebuchadnezzar destroyed Jerusalem, the temple, and took the population into exile in Babylon. Date 587 BC!

That cleared, back to John Williams' anthem and Harrison Ford cracking his whip!

Dear *To Sir with Love*,

You are a film with great warmth and charm, especially considering that you are a film about education, about teaching difficult students in a difficult school in the London Docklands, a black teacher amongst mainly white students, the 1960s.

But I want to tell you a story about how significant you were (my not realising it at the time) in setting me off on the path of film reviewing. During 1967, my confrere and friend, Paul Stenhouse, editor of *Annals Australia*, featured some background articles and photos on religious films of the period, especially Pasolini's *The Gospel According to St Matthew* and Robert Bolt's play, *A Man for All Seasons*. It had occurred to me that it would be good idea to have film reviews in *Annals*. And then I saw you in Melbourne. You hadn't been released yet in Sydney and a press preview was advertised. That event, and you, were the catalysts for my first review – and, a touch of publicity, we were all given an apple as we entered the theatrette!

Seeing you twice within a month was a pleasure. You are a very appealing film, a film of great humanity. I was certainly ready to empathise with you because I was coming to the conclusion of a year and a quarter teaching in our Canberra high school, not anticipating that that was where I would be going after ordination and being asked to stay on for an extra year. I soon realised that working in a high school in 1966-1967 (not so easy in looking back at the atmosphere of those times, more freedoms, emerging drug use, the Vietnam war and conscription) enabled me to get my feet on the ground, so to speak, dealing with teenage boys, discovering their abilities, encountering their problems, discussions with their parents.

Of course, it would have been rather nice to have been a Sidney Poitier-type teacher but who of us has his calm demeanour, even when riled, and his empathy with his students, despite the rebellious moments? But your title does give away the thrust of the drama and I still see and hear the scenes of Sidney Poitier walking amongst the students, their final admiration, and there was a Lulu singing so plaintively, 'To Sir with Love...'.

In looking back, I realise now as I did not at the time, that your release in 1967 was only four years after the March on Washington and Martin Luther King's 'I have a dream...'. Sidney Poitier had won the Best Acting Oscar for *Lilies of the Field* in that archetypal year, 1963. And, here he was, three very significant films released in 1967, yourself, then declaring 'They call me Mr Tibbs' in *In the Heat of the Night*, and the mixed-race marriage of *Guess Who's Coming to Dinner*. And then I remembered that director Stanley Kramer had used Poitier almost ten years earlier for a racial challenge, Poitier cuffed to Tony Curtis, prison escapees in *The Defiant Ones*. (And, as I write to you, he is still living at age 91.)

You had some excellent credits. The screenplay was based on a book by teacher E. A. Braithwaite, built on his teaching experiences in a London school. You were a rare directing job by novelist James Clavell, *Shogun* and a religious history film that I liked very much, *The Last Valley*. There were emerging stars of the time – Judy Geeson, Suzy Kendall, Lulu – and, there on the staff was Hyacinth Buckett (Bouquet)/Hetty Winthrop, Patricia Routledge herself – and I was fortunate to see her later on the London stage pontificating as Lady Bracknell!

I thought I should finish with a quote from my first official film review, in January 1968:

> (*To Sir with Love*)... shows a teacher grappling with the problems of education and solving them when he treats the children as potential adults, as human beings who respond to kindness, sympathy and real goals and values. The average teacher could not hope to emulate the success of Poitier's Mark Thackeray, but will get a big lift from watching this story and this performance.

A wistful comment based on experience.

Dear *Inception*,

Conception? Deception? Exception? Perception? Reception? All of the above, plus Inception. That is how I began my review of you. I was wondering what to think – because I was very taken by your plot and themes, your dream themes. You are a science-fiction exploration of the psyche.

When I told my good friend, Jan Epstein, that I was writing to you, she said that her choice would be to write to *Interstellar*, her favourite Christopher Nolan film. I realised that for years she has enjoyed reading contemporary science books whereas I preferred psychological themes. For her, *Interstellar* is a great science/fantasy/fiction exploration of space and time. I prefer to go inwards, into the imagination, into dreams.

I think you are a film certainly about 'reality', but all the time asking the question, 'what is reality?' or 'how many realities can exist at the same time?'. We usually say that we can't bilocate even though there are plenty of stories of parallel worlds, of time travel and doppelgangers. With *Inception* and its exploration of dreams and the variety of dream worlds, we can actually bilocate (or, as here, trilocate and, even, quatrolocate) because we can by lying asleep while active in our dreams. And, as posited here, in dreams within dreams!

I hope you don't mind me now thinking aloud. Because we all dream and are fascinated by our dream selves and behaviours, the audience generally goes willingly into the world of Inception. When we speak about our imagination and drives in both waking and dreaming states, we start to use the language of the sub-conscious which emerges and the unconscious which is driving us unawares. Characters in dreams are facets of ourselves and projections from our sub-conscious, revealing deeper aspects of our psyches and personalities than we might be willing to share when awake. There is plenty of verbal exposition of these themes in your screenplay but, more importantly, we see these themes illustrated in the complex stories and dreams.

Just thinking, I hope you're with me.

Whether all that we see is possible in reality is debatable. It seems scientifically implausible if not impossible – but who knows whether in years, decades or centuries, medical, scientific and psychological techniques will combine to make some of this actual! Then we think of the development of brainwashing techniques, truth drugs and cult leaders' mind control of followers. And, all the time, there is the unpredictable human factor, something which Inception explores in its dreams.

Could I take the opportunity to sort out something of the approach of the plot? The opening is puzzling as Leonardo di Caprio's Cobb is washed ashore and brought before an elderly Japanese businessman in his exotic house. We arrive back here at the end, discovering what state of consciousness it is, but the flashbacks begin explaining Cobb and his team and their capacity to enter the dreams of others, their being awake in the dreams, and able to extract information that can be used for good or for ill. Cobb has become an ideas' thief. We see dreams within dreams at once but our puzzle is working out who is dreaming – and who is in who's dream. Since Cobb has gone beyond ethical bounds which has cost him his wife and his children, he is consumed by memories of her and her unanticipated presence in his dreams. He wants to redeem himself and move from thieving extraction of information from dreams to inception, the inserting of ideas in dreams so that the dreamer might think that the incepted (the correct word?) idea (which is compared to a virus) is self-generated rather than implanted.

Inside the dreams, we get plenty of action where audiences might think they are in an adaptation of a graphic novel (including a vast snow episode that outdoes James Bond and films like *On Her Majesty's Secret Service*). In fact, there is a great deal of action amidst the speculations. The locations are also filmed quite spectacularly, with action set in Japan, Paris, Kenya and Los Angeles. And the effects are sometimes amazing, especially the city of Paris folding on itself and, while a van containing the sleeping team falls in slowest motion from a bridge into a river with Joseph Gordon Levitt's Arthur being rocked by the fall and having to perform deadline feats of saving the team who are also asleep in a hotel in another dream by defying gravity. I am tempted to add: Whew!

And, of course, the final question: is how you end in reality? After all, we are participating in a waking dream as well as watching the reality and unreality on screen.

Christopher Nolan has shown himself no slouch in making films that demand attention: *Memento* a decade earlier with its action moving backwards in time, the Arctic thriller, *Insomnia*, his three Batman films, *Batman Begins*, *The Dark Knight*, *The Dark Knight Rises*, his intriguing tale of rival magicians, *The Prestige*, *Interstellar* then rather coming down-to-earth, *Dunkirk*. His next film sounds tantalising, *Tenet*, described as 'an action epic revolving around international espionage, time travel, and evolution'. And, tenet is a palindrome – in my end is my beginning!

Nolan is obviously enjoying this opportunity to write and direct your screenplay that is quite outside the box while guiding a fine cast doing their best and playing with special effects to his heart's – and our hearts' and imaginations' – content.

Dear *Joker*,

I have to say I was very much taken by you, drawn into your portrait of Arthur Fleck, Joker-to-be. Critics seem to be divided about you, which surprised me, because you had just won the Golden Lion in Venice. In fact, I was quite irritated (on your behalf as well as in myself) by the review in our major Melbourne paper. It seemed to me a review by derision, which is rather petty now that I think of it. There were many derogatory comments, less rather than more relevant, about your director, Todd Phillips, 'brazenly low-brow' because of his *Eurotrip* and *Hangover* series. 'Making a career out of manchild movies and here is another'.

As I write, the nominations for film awards for 2019 have not been announced. And, I should mention that I've never written a letter to a film in the DC world or the Marvel Universe but I felt a kind of compulsion, even as I watched you, to write to you.

But let tell you an anecdote. The other day, I had an ECG and the technician asked whether I had seen you. She and her partner had. I was just about to say that for me you are a film about mental illness but she got in first with the same idea. For me, you are a very powerful case study of extremes in mental illness. It is hard not to feel sorry for Arthur so much of the time – his intense introspection, the disturbing maniacal neurological laugh and his difficulty in controlling it, erupting at all the wrong moments. That laugh will be one of the main features that will stay in my memory.

But, of course, with the name *Joker*, it is the clown imagery and metaphor that drew me in.

The first time we see Arthur, he is pulling his lips apart to grin. He is not a natural laughter clown. Then he grimaces, the sad clown. Then I realised he is bereft, an orphaned clown, an institutionalised clown, a medicated clown. Where he succeeds best is in some sympathetic rapport with children. Where he fails, despite his scrawly and sketchy book of jokes, his attempts to tell them, is in his embarrassing gig as a stand-up comic in the club. As his mother remarks, 'Don't you have to be funny to be a comedian?'. And this is the experience, unexpectedly videoed, played for mockery on television, that leads to his downfall.

Most commentators have remembered that Robert De Niro had a similar kind of role and aspiration in Scorsese's *King of Comedy*. Now, De Niro has achieved his ambitions as the TV host who is ultimately merciless to Arthur though he agrees to introduce him as Joker.

At the beginning, I wondered whether there would be any reference to Bruce Wayne or the Wayne family. As you progressed, I was very impressed with the dramatic, gradual way you opened up the family, mention of the name, the chaos in Gotham City and Thomas Wayne campaigning to be mayor, then the revelation about Penny Fleck working at the Wayne Mansion, suspicions about her pregnancy, about Arthur's paternity, issues of adoption, Arthur's search for documentation and his visit to the mansion, encountering Alfred and the young Bruce, and the issues of Penny herself and her obsession with Thomas Wayne and her illusions. But I certainly didn't expect the sequence where Arthur ultimately, and shockingly, deals with his mother.

Which brings up the question of your violence. While we see Arthur/Joker in action, we have to remember the hardships of his upbringing and his uncertainties, the mental state of his mother, his own illness and neurological laugh, the sequence where the young men bullied him in the street, the yuppie mockery in the subway train, the injustice of his boss firing him, the mockery from the other clown who gave him the gun – which means that Arthur became a 'punishing clown'. A touch of kindness to the dwarf who never mocked him. But then, calling Murray to account on television, punishment by execution.

And then I remember that this is an 'Origins' story, not the usual origins of the superheroes but rather the origin of Batman's most notorious foe – which reminds us of Jack Nicholson's maniacal glee and the more deadly notorious (and Oscar-winning) hostile madness of Heath Ledger. Of course, we are not meant to identify with Arthur's and Joker's increasing brutality. That would be a sign of mental illness. Rather, Gotham city is decaying, and Arthur is part of that decay.

Of course, Arthur/Joker's impact is in the writing, the director and his use of intense close-ups and framing, but the tribute must go to Joaquin Phoenix, emaciated, quietly and then openly deranged, lacking any sense of humour though desiring it, wanting an identity, donning make up (covering Arthur for a new identity), wearing masks to hide but running the risk of their being torn off his face and his being recognised. It is a significant performance – and you are a significant film, contributing to and critiquing 21st-century culture.

Dear *The Insult/ L'Insulte*,

You are the first Lebanese film I have written to. I reviewed you on your release as a film to be recommended and you were Lebanon's Oscar nomination for Best Foreign Language film 2017.

Your title is very straightforward. And, in some ways, so is the incident which leads to the insult but does not anticipate many of the dire consequences. I read the interviews with your director where he explained that his screenplay was based on an actual incident, and that it involved himself, an outburst of criticism and insult to a plumber. He said that the consequences were certainly not as he expected and they made quite some demands on him for reconciliation – but it provided personal experience on which to base a screenplay which takes the insult much further.

It is not necessary to know a great deal of the history of Lebanon in recent decades to appreciate this film. I've seen a number of films since, Israeli films, Lebanese films, American which highlight the cultural and religious differences, the Civil War. In fact, with that in mind, I did visit Lebanon in 2003 and 2006 for my Catholic Cinema work. And I really did enjoy the visits, the welcoming people, travelling to the Cedars, to the Bekaa Valley, down to the border with Israel (remembering that I had stood on the other side in 1979 and that there was no way across either time). I certainly learnt about Lebanon's history. We even drove in a minibus to Damascus and around Western Syria – and, three weeks later, heard that the Beirut airport had been bombed as had the road to Syria. And later, an American customs official declared himself unhappy with my having Lebanon, Syria, Iran visits in my passport, 'Why have you got that?'!

But, back to you, something of an allegory of resentments, hatreds, angers and conflicts in the Middle East. However, you introduce immediately a militant Christian group in Lebanon and its fierce loyalties, as well as a background of hate talk on the radio. Your central character, Tony, is a garage mechanic in Beirut, a Christian area which contrasts with the Palestinian camps. Your other character is Yasser, a Palestinian refugee, living in a camp, a generally calm man who is supervising building sites with great success and finesse.

The insult incident is so trivial in many ways, Tony hosing his balcony, an open pipe spilling water onto passers-by. Yasser confronts Tony, tries to fix the pipe, Tony smashing it, leading to a verbal confrontation, provocative because of the hate messages on the radio, and a punch which leads to broken ribs in hospital. Tony demands an apology of Yasser. Yasser is not prepared to give it.

This part of the drama is interesting in itself, the director creating (and remembering) quite a sense of tension, Tony absolutely fixed and rigid in his stances and prejudices, Yasser remaining calm but then provoked.

As I watched, I was surprised that so much of your action actually takes place in the court as Tony decides to sue Yasser. You certainly become more complex when a top Beirut lawyer, Christian, interviews Tony and prepares a spirited and somewhat bigoted prosecution of Yasser. Your irony is that Yasser's defence lawyer is the daughter of the prosecutor, her first case, quite a rivalry. There are three judges who preside – and the trial proceeds with interrogation of witnesses but spontaneous interventions from both lawyers.

The trial gives an opportunity for the audience to appreciate something of what is behind the hostility, the experience of the Palestinians, the behaviour of Israel, the role of the PLO, the refugees in camps in Lebanon. But it also gives the opportunity to appreciate the experience of the civil war in Lebanon in the 1970s, the role of PLO and Palestinians, massacres in Christian villages and still-unresolved animosities.

You are very involving drama, audiences off-put by the angry Tony, appreciating the calmness of Yasser (and the introduction of complications of Yasser's behaviour when he was a young man in the camps and involved in violence). You ask of your audience very serious thought about the conflicts in the Middle East, what is behind them, and possible solutions for peace if not reconciliation.

You are a sober reminder that trivial matters could lead to catastrophe.

Dear *Judy and Punch*,

You were very much a surprise, with some moments of shock, a real-life Punch and Judy show at a press preview at 9.30 in the morning. Quite a way to start a day. You were not what I expected at all and, at the end, I was in some admiration but still with some shock.

One of the first things I realised was that I knew nothing of the origins of Punch and Judy shows. So, off to that information shortcut, Wikipedia. I had been wondering what century, what year you were set in and, immediately, there was the answer, England 1662, the beginning of the Restoration period, some influence from Italian shows, especially the character of Puncianello, a marionette entertainment.

Of course, like everyone else, I have seen some actual Punch and Judy shows as well as seeing them during action in various films. There were the main two characters, literally sparring with each other, most of the memories being of each of them with what looked like a baseball bat having goes at each other. And I think I remember the devil. But I don't remember the crocodile. But I do remember that children generally enjoyed the show, rollicking with laughter, even at the violence.

So, you are a film of origins. And, obviously, your writer and director, Mirrah Foulkes, wanted to make a point about the inherent misogyny in the shows. You name Mia Waskiowski's Judy first rather than Punch. (And I had already seen Damon Herriman as Charles Manson via Quentin Tarantino, smilingly sinister.) And so it is their story your screenplay weaves, touches of fantasy, touches of the supernatural and superstition, touches of myth, more than a touch of misogyny, a portrait of a very unpleasant community.

I suppose you are a fable about the village and the people in the village. I suppose you are a parable, inviting us into a world which, at first, we might seem to know, but then subverting all the expectations of how the village and the villagers should live. You are shrewd in inviting us to follow the young girl, Scout, through the darkness to the village walls, past the women of the night, into the tavern, settling in to watch the entertainment, Judy wandering among the rough clients, impoverished, both men and women, trying to collect some coins. And then Punch, introducing himself, vanishing with a puff of smoke behind the curtain, with Judy and Punch and the skilled puppeteering of their show. Judy declares that it is rather violent, Punch replying that that was what the audience wanted.

So, there we were in rural England of the 17th century, soon discovering that like their cousins across the Atlantic later in Salem and other towns, there was a fierce religiosity, belief in the devil and evil rather than in goodness and God, experiences of sin and, what often follows with allegedly good people, finding scapegoats on which to load malevolent burdens. Then you show an ousted community, mainly of women, condemned as witches. And the morose villagers eager for public denunciations, stonings and hangings, with Punch casting the first stone, certainly not innocent.

Your scene of Punch tripping and the baby flying out the window to its death will stay in my memory as an image of offhand violence, Punch not only not grieving but ready for a cover-up, scapegoating the two elderly servants in the house, beating his wife to death and burying her in the forest.

A Punch and Judy show in real life.

Which meant that you had me hooked, Judy surely not dead, relief that Scout found her in the woods, intrigued by the women exiled as witches, healing power, welcoming Judy to community, but a community of no fixed abode. I remember feeling vengeful on Judy's behalf.

And I remember feeling morose delight how Judy taunted and tormented Punch during the storm, her cloak hanging in the lightning light as a diabolical presence. I was grieved at Punch's malice in sacrificing the servants, and then his rationalising, like so many self-righteous, allegedly religious people, telling the vindictive crowd, eager for the hangings, that he was not guilty but it was the devil through the servants. And the crowd was relieved that the hangings could go on, Punch himself pulling the lever and – relief, the ropes slashed, the servants saved.

At the moment, I'm re-living Judy riding into town, somersaulting on to the gallows, her rousing speech of accusation, Punch raising his hands – and the slash. A padded cell, Punch's hell on earth, and the macabre moment of Punch and Judy, cloth faces on his arms' stumps.

I know you end with peace in the village, justice done, the women in exile coming back to the town, settling down, future peace. And I appreciated your collection of black and white pictures of children in the audience of Punch and Judy shows. But, that has not stayed in my memory, it is Punch madly puppeteering with those macabre stumps.

Dear *The Report*,

(or would you rather prefer the full title, *The Torture Report*, but with the word 'Torture' redacted with whiteout as happens during your opening credit – redaction being rather significant for you?)

You are the kind of film that I would enjoy seeing at any time. The intricacies of politics, especially American politics, are always intriguing. And, come to think of it, it does not take very long after the events for behind-the-scenes intrigues and machinations to become the theme of popular films – though, come to think of it again, it was only two years between Nixon's resignation and *All the President's Men*. In more recent years, there have been *W*, *Vice*, *Zero Dark Thirty*. *Fair Game*.

But, what made you even more significant for me, is that I was reviewing you in the very weeks that the impeachment of Donald Trump was being voted on. (I know that there have been so many references to Donald Trump in recent films, comic criticism rather than political analysis, and that he definitely looks and sounds like Alec Baldwin in *Saturday Night Live*.)

When I re-read this letter in years to come, I will know the answer to the issue of the impeachment and whether or not Donald Trump had a second term in the presidency.

In the meantime, here is the CIA, the exercise of torture from 2002 in the wake of 9/11 and the war against terror until 2008 and its being banned by President Obama. When you think about it – and there was plenty of thinking about it while I watched you – I was glad that I was being made to realise how much goes on behind the scenes, in the various departments, in the Congress, in the White House, the number of documents, the reports, the redactions, secrecy and security, personal rivalries, protecting of jobs and reputations, increasing carelessness of and/or admitting or covering the truth.

If anybody asked me what would be a good film to try to understand what might have been going on during Donald Trump's initial years, the investigation into Russian interference, the frequent resignations of officials in the administration, the events which led to impeachment, you would be my first recommendation.

I would like to commend Adam Driver and his performance as investigator Daniel Jones, listed as an advisor for you. He is the embodiment of an intensely principled American, completely dedicated to his work (but no real personal life to speak of), tempted to be a whistleblower, disgusted with the coverups, relentless in his examination of documents, making connections, wanting the truth to be told no matter what. Which is where Annette Bening's excellent performance as Senator Diane Feinstein from California needs to be seen as something of counterbalance. Not that she did not want truth to be revealed, but she was very conscious in her political life of the need for shrewd decision-making and the implications and consequences of politicking. (One of the reasons I was particularly interested in seeing Diane Feinstein was that I travelled back into my past, a quarter term at the Graduate Theological Union in Berkeley at the end of 1978, being in California at the time of Jonestown and its horrors, and the assassination of the San Francisco mayor and the adviser, Harvey Milk – the subject of Gus van Sant's, *Milk*, with Sean Penn – an eye-and-consciousness-opening for me, the first time living in the US.)

You have a reference to *Zero Dark Thirty* and the CIA information which led to the attack on Osama Bin Laden. That film also had scenes of torture, bringing to our consciousness the issue and violence of waterboarding. In your early sequences, you do not hold back on indicating the range of tortures that were permitted, the limited medical con-men who sold the CIA on torture, and the vast amount of money spent on it, and the very limited information on future terrorist attacks that it elicited from the victims. As with the torture, there are the grim scenes where CIA officials rather callously watch and concur in the torture, using the principle that the end justifies the means.

There is also a reference to Edward Snowden (remembering Oliver Stone's portrait of *Snowden*) and we think of Julian Assange and Chelsea Manning, a reminder of some of the truths that they revealed and official deceptions played on the American public and on the world's public.

As they say in the promotion of a mystery film, novel or play, 'All will be revealed'. The revelation may not be immediate but, with communications so complex these days, with human motivation so entangled, but with the hope that there is integrity in truth, so much will be revealed sooner rather than later.

PS. You don't require back-up, but a week after you were released, we saw *Official Secrets* from Britain, involving documents and intrigue behind the scenes in both Britain and the US, a whistleblower leaking secrets concerning the claim of weapons of mass destruction before the 2003 invasion of Iraq.

Dear *Mrs Lowry and Son*,

I was drawn into you immediately and, by the time the final credits came, you were high on my list of enjoyments for the year. It was wonderful to watch the reactions, interactions between Vanessa Redgrave and Timothy Spall as mother and son – not always relaxing and lovey-dovey, often harsh and humiliating on her side, sometimes crushed submission on his.

It is not always an advantage to preview a film on one's computer with a Vimeo link but this was the setup for watching you and, very soon, I was very glad. It was when Mrs Lowry gruffly referred to her son as a 'vexation' that I realised that the screenplay, by Martyn Hesford from his play, was rich in vocabulary, articulate in expression, arresting in its use of words, the words bringing the performances even more alive. And I realised that this was Vanessa Redgrave at her best as Mrs Lowry (and, for fifty years, she has frequently been at her best) and that this was Timothy Spall at his best (also to be seen at his best in Mike Leigh films, *Secrets and Lies*, *All or Nothing*, *Another Year* and his interpretation of the painter, *Mr Turner*).

And, with this realisation, I decided to take notes, to highlight on my page the word choices, the expressions, those touches of phrase that keep us alert as well as delight us.

I thought you might like to be reminded of some of them.

The words are mainly those of Mrs Lowry. Her son, very meek and mild, even co-dependent with his mother, did not have all that much to say except that he painted what he saw and what he felt, that he was called to paint. And, as the film went on, he was at the receiving end of his mother's cruelty, his mother's snobbery, her narcissism, her lifelong growing in disdain for all that she did not approve of, her disappointment in life.

I jotted down that I wondered whether, in that small room where most of the action takes place, her bedroom, where she is in fact bedridden, was her safe place, alone in her safe world. I also wondered whether she was frailly-strong or strongly-frail. But she relished being snugly bed-ridden and secluded.

In fact, though quietly spoken, removed from most reality (except newspapers and her son's conversation), she is monstrous towards her son and has been for decades. She relishes the harsh criticism by the local art critic of one of her son's paintings, automatically believing the critic because he knows as a critic and not her son because he is a merely would-be artist. Her comment on his now-famous painting of workers leaving the mill, is 'You find that beautiful, nobody else does'. And she offers her harsh comments quite airily, her point of view being always right, no consideration for her son let alone sympathy. Empathy is not a consideration. She says she has no interests in life's deformities, his paintings are embarrassing, she prefers the picturesque, the tasteful, pictures of nice things. Even thinking about a mill that she has never seen is abhorrent.

There is a scene where, surprisingly, she does like one of his paintings. But that is because her neighbour, something of a mirror-image of Mrs Lowry as she clashes with her own husband, tells his mother that she likes this painting. It is one of sailing. She remembers the occasion in one of the many flashbacks to her young days, the beginnings of her disappointment in her husband, her wanting to be a pianist, not getting the life she imagined, nor the house and area to live in that she yearned for.

As regards the picture of the mill, she remarks that 'we can see that every day and what will be the point of painting this!'

When her son receives an encouraging letter from a London entrepreneur, she is more interested that it came from London than it is about his art. In a moment of wilful selfishness, she tears up his letter, scatters the pieces, ignores his disappointment as he collates the pieces. He goes up and starts to smash the paintings in the attic, gathering them in the yard to burn them – and, as they quietly and casually eat their next meal, she enquires about the burning, fully expecting that it happened and that it should have happened.

And so, sitting all the time in her bed, capitalising on moments of frailty, eating her son's prepared meals with eager munching, she regrets having a son, disappointed by her husband, she is an image of a callous monster, completely oblivious of her capacity for destruction. I have to tell you that I'd never heard of L. S. Lowry or his art – but there was a sense of satisfaction in seeing the 21st-century exhibitions at the end, the range and style of his painting, and the recognition in the screenplay by having him sit amongst the viewers in the gallery. And, sadly, his final comment that he had done all his paintings for his mother.

Dear *I Still See You*,

You may well be surprised that you are receiving a letter from me. My friends will also be surprised that I'm writing you this letter. I am not sure that you received a commercial release in Australia and I came across you on the Foxtel Thrillers Channel. I appreciate that you are a small-budget film, probably destined for a popular audience on television or through streaming.

So, I should explain to you why I am writing.

You are a genre film. In fact, you combine two genres: there is the search for a serial killer; there is your science-fiction setting. And so the truth for me to admit is, I do enjoy genre films and appreciate the conventions (realising that many moviegoers think that genre films are lesser films – and, often enough, they are). When I realised that I had enjoyed watching you, I thought I'd better check out the bloggers on the IMDb (a varied and sometimes fickle group of correspondents, from vicious trolls to hearty enthusiasts). If you hadn't heard, you will be pleased that most were very favourable – and I agreed with them.

One thought was that if a big commercial company had taken on your basic screenplay, developed it and its themes, used a cast of well-known actors and multiplied the special effects, you would have made something of an entertaining blockbuster. But that was not to be. You don't waste any time in setting your pace. The introduction to your focal character, Veronica, as a little girl, her parents – and then, their certainly being taken unawares by a shockwave and its devastating effect, more than a touch apocalyptic, on those who lived around Chicago. Then, instantly, ten years later.

We discover that the apocalypse was not quite as apocalyptic as we had imagined. And this is where your theme does become very interesting as we watch Veronica, 'Ronnie', a wilful and sometimes disturbed teenager, having breakfast with her parents, her father reading the paper at the table, a cup of coffee – his smile and his wistfully dissolving and disappearing.

On her way to school, riding her bike, Ronnie sees neighbours watering the garden – and dissolving. She rides into an elderly lady who also dissolves. A group of students at school, chatting, also disappear. So, what is this science-fiction theme?

What is interesting is that the class that Ronnie attends, distracted, given by Mr Bittner, is about these characters who appear and disappear, remnants of their past existence, caught at a particular moment of their lives, to be repeated and repeated over and over again. The device of the screenplay is to tantalise us with the rules about 'Rems', the fact of their survival, a link between life and death and life, their not intervening in human lives or communicating with the living. Just appearing and disappearing. 'I still see you'. Well, not quite – and this leads into the other genre, murders and a search for the murderer.

A mysterious character, Brian, appears when Ronnie is showering and writes 'Run' in the steam on her mirror. And she keeps seeing him, at sports events, and again in her bathroom. What emerges is that Brian is associated with the disappearance of a young woman. Ronnie, and her friend, Kirk, discover more and more, researching newspapers and stories, interviewing people associated with the young woman, discovering that there have been further deaths. And here come the conventions, the birthdays of the victims occurring on February 29th – as, of course, we discover that this is Ronnie's birthday and that she is under murderous threat.

Then more on the apocalyptic, Ronnie and Kirk going to Ground Zero of the explosion and shock, a dark abandoned area, the remains of the laboratories and underground tunnels, peopled with a vast number of Rems, but also a number of live people – including the remorseful scientist responsible for the shockwave, giving science-fiction fans plenty to think about in his explanation of the aims of the project, finding a door between life and death and the afterlife, but opening a far more overwhelming connection than anticipated.

As your pace increases, you become even more interesting, the discovery that Brian was an assistant at the plant, and then the revelation that Mr Bittner was the associate and lost his daughter in the shockwave, and her reappearing to him as a Rem. And more excitement as the pace revs up, Mr Bittner preparing a panic room isolation so that Ronnie won't be affected on her birthday, Kirk discovering the truth, Mr Bittner attempting to bury him, Ronnie escaping, going to the frozen lake where her father had taught her as a little girl to skate – and, of course, we know from seeing her dreams (and seeing these conventions in other films) that the ice will crack and open, Mr Bittner submerged and the Rem of her father rescuing her.

Audiences with a more elitist sensibility are prone to poke fun at the inevitability and what they condemn as predictability of the conventions. Genre fans relish the conventions and how they are used and their variations. As you can see from this letter, I belong to the latter group.

While I watched you, I thought you were being more inventive concerning shockwaves, deaths, remnants and ghosts, threats and retribution than the average popular show.

Thanks for an interesting and entertaining ninety-eight minutes.

Dear *The Professor and his Beloved Equation*,

It is over a decade since I saw you and memories of your plot and its details, the impact of your visuals, have faded. However, I still remember the where and when I saw you and your effect on me. I would like to let you know but, first, let me say something about maths. You are a film about mathematics, the delight of your central character, the Professor. And you are a Japanese film, immersed in the culture, immersed in Japanese society.

We all had to do arithmetic back in the good old days, then some sections on algebra, and also some geometry. I was alright with the subjects but they weren't my favourites. In the latter part of secondary school, I was persuaded to keep doing maths even for the final exams, a subject described as General Maths. And I did get an A. I don't know what the effect of doing maths for five years in secondary school has had – probably some development of a different disciplined way of thinking and interpreting reality.

I meant to mention earlier that, in our first year in secondary school, our teacher, Father Sheridan, was shrewd in motivating us, setting us tasks, problems to be solved, and the promise of his reading one of G. K. Chesterton's Fr Brown stories. In fact, this was excellent motivation!

Speaking of teachers, that's how you open, an enthusiastic young man entering a classroom and beginning to tell his students the story of the professor and his influence on the young teacher.

I am presuming that not many readers of these letters will have seen you. And so my plea: Please do not be put off by the title. If the potential audience had heard that a film with a title like this was about numbers, mathematics, equations, memory loss and baseball, they might well be puzzled. But that is who you are – and you have to be one of the nicest (in the best sense) films in a long time.

As I have mentioned, you open with students settling down to a maths class with their new teacher. He introduces himself and proceeds to entrance the class and the cinema audience with the story of how he came to be a maths teacher. It involves his single mother who worked for a housekeeping agency and was given the task of looking after a maths professor who had been in a car accident and has now lost the memory of all that happened after the accident (except for eighty minutes' retention before it disappears and he has to start again but keeps notes during his lucidity for further reference and study). This mother is a good woman, devout, devoted, listens eagerly to the professor's theories about amicable numbers, prime numbers, perfect numbers and how maths is interior and is a revelation of truth.

She also brings her ten-year-old son who is coached by the professor in maths – and then in baseball, which is the sport the professor played when young and which he loves (and remembers all the pre-accident statistics). His sister-in-law, who was made lame by the same accident, is an embittered woman and tries to sabotage the friendship.

While this is an overview of 'what happens', it does not do justice to the 'how it happens'. Your performances are rich and rewarding, perfectly credible. The deep humanity and joy that pervades your storytelling has a wonderful effect on the audience's sense of goodness. There is enough dialogue to suggest the transcendent and the infinite in our world, with the quotation from Blake about the world in a grain of sand and the professor noting that he has been 'allowed to peep into God's notebook'.

The film, beautiful to look at, especially with ocean, water, mountains and blossoms, is in the classic tradition of contemplative naturalistic filming of the master Japanese director, Ozu.

I had better finish by mentioning the where and when I saw you. For several years, I had the good fortune to be part of the interfaith jury in Tehran at the Fajr Festival. I have to add that the welcome in Tehran, the screening of so many films with human values, even at the time when President George Bush was including Iran in his 'axis of evil', my memories of being in Iran are very happy. And, surprisingly, in 2005, a decision was made for the Fajr Festival that they would include a section, Spirituality Cinema. I was on the jury for that section of the festival twice. I would have to also add that the criteria for films for this section were puzzling. The selection included Japanese ghost stories! There was little discussion about to whom we would award the 2008 prize – you.

I think you have been little seen outside Japan. Somebody remarked that you were screened on air flights. But I tried to do my best when I reviewed you. The other good thing was that an Iranian television channel invited me to be interviewed, to explain why we gave you our award. It was in English. I did my best to enthusiastically commend you. I never saw the footage, my one big opportunity to be involved in local Farsi culture!

I did highlight my conclusion that you were well-worth seeing and reflecting on.

Dear *Black Narcissus*,

I first saw you forty plus years ago, intrigued because of your subject, the community of nuns in the Himalayas, but wanting to think about the issues because, in those years, I had a role in the formation of the men joining my religious congregation – obviously watching you with a 'compare and contrast' attitude towards your characters and the men that I was working with.

Now, a re-viewing after about forty-five years. I'm still interested in the compare and contrast. But also in the nature of the experience of a religious call, the experience of living a vocation, the quality of commitment, the motivation for mission.

Even on my television screen, Jack Cardiff's colour photography is extraordinarily bright and vivid. And there is the reminder, surprising as it is, that filming was done at Pinewood Studios, no Indian locations. Yet up there on the screen you seem absolutely authentic, the majesty of the Himalayas, the convent on the chasm top, the lush undergrowth in the valleys, the life of the locals, the exotic and extensive art on the walls. Extraordinary production design that makes us feel we are really there.

I thought I should look up Rumer Godden before writing this letter to you: her early years in India, her publishing the novel, *Black Narcissus*, in 1939, so echoing the experiences of the 1930s. I see she wrote many novels, many of them adapted for the screen – the one that I remember, nuns again, this time Catholic Benedictines, *In This House of Brede*. Then I noticed that she had been interested in Catholicism for many years and finally became a Catholic in 1968. So, much authentic background.

When you were first released and even in the decades following, most audiences were not familiar with Anglican nuns, the style of

Anglo-Catholicism and the strong parallels with Roman Catholicism – but now everybody seems to be familiar with Anglican nuns after several series of *Call the Midwife*! For those not immediately in the know, your nuns could be quickly interpreted as Catholic. (But then there was the chance to see Deborah Kerr as a Catholic nun, marooned with Robert Mitchum in *Heaven Knows Mr Allison*, in 1956.)

But back to the religious community and trying to appreciate how it ticked. First of all, it is interesting to note that the focus is on the nuns, that there is no priest, no chaplain, no male religious adviser even though there is a Chapel with an altar. The regional superior in India has all the authority, assigning sisters to the new foundation, her decision alone. And, this is tricky because you explain that the sisters renew their vows every year, that the community does not rely on a sense of stability or permanency. And we see this in the moodiness and mental disturbance in Sister Ruth as well as the more sympathetic and elderly gardener, Sister Philippa, who is becoming more and more lost in her interior world. So far, so interesting.

But what does your screenplay indicate about vocation? The way that the sisters speak, especially Sister Clodagh, is often very cerebral – that vocation is something of a Christian ideology, commitment to a cause rather than a deep and growing personal relationship with Jesus Christ and with God. The God language of the screenplay harkens back to more traditional and doctrinal times. Sister Clodagh communicates this by word but the directors have been very careful in getting Deborah Kerr to act subtly during her silences, her observations, the reactions in her eyes, facial quivers that indicate the mixture of authority and turmoil in her interior life. She is strict but also tries to be caring. To be in charge is important for her although it isolates her in a certain loneliness. She tries to be authentic but this is measured by her religious codes rather than a personal and personalised spirituality.

The nuns pray. They say religious things. They are best seen, however, in their ministry outreach, to the young girls coming to learn, the articulate young boy who speaks English and interprets, to the young prince and his earnest curriculum. This is particularly true of the young sister, Sister Honey, who is not cerebral at all, but lovingly cheerful in her outreach, upset at the consequences of her dealing with a village mother and her dying child.

Of course, in the cinema world – but even more of course, in the actual world – there is the perennial theme of celibacy, sexual attraction, emotional conflict, authenticity and principles and commitment.

Despite the wind howling continually on the mountain top that seems to affect everyone, the local agent, a rather debonair David Farrar, is usually seen wearing shorts and, often, shirtless. And so, throughout your action, there is the effect of the male presence on all the Sisters, sending Sister Clodagh into flashbacks of her past, her love, eventually being jilted, her consequent going into the convent as a reaction, although she explains it as God moving in mysterious ways. And much more melodramatic is the effect on Sister Ruth, her sending out to buy a burgundy dress, her wearing it, her imposing herself on the agent, his rejection, mad behaviour and look, the attack on Sister Clodagh, falling down the chasm cliff. Plenty of symbolism and objective co-relatives there! (And in the background, and sometimes in the foreground, is the young woman played by Jean Simmons who is not interested in learning but enjoys tantalising the young prince.)

I realise I should be stopping and that there is little space in this letter for points like the colonial attitudes of the Sisters towards the locals, that you were released in the year of Partition, the contrast with missionary activity in Africa or the countries of the Pacific, the failure of the mission and its impact on the people and the Sisters themselves. Maybe I will get the chance to write you another letter and follow through with these themes. But, for now, many thanks.

Dear *Fargo*,

I keep wondering why you resonated so well with audiences in the middle of the 1990s, as the 20th century came to an end. And I keep wondering why I enjoyed seeing you so much.

Two things come to mind immediately. First, there is the wonderful performance by Frances McDormand as Marge Gunderson (with an Oscar to prove it), the heavily pregnant sheriff of Brainerd (with its snowbound statue of the pioneer on the highway), the North Dakota and Minnesota population with their heavy accents drawing on their inherited Scandinavian intonations. I know everyone is entitled to their accent and that we know that we ourselves have no accent (and everyone else declares that they have no accent), but the intonations and rhythms certainly get our attention and tickle touches of humour. And Marge is so down-to-earth, comfortable always with her supportive husband, doing police work with efficiency, sometimes plodding, sometimes ingenious, making it all sound logical, interrupting her work with hearty meals, driving earnestly through the snow, and giving it all her full commitment, 'ya'. I hope Frances McDormand agrees with that!

The second point is the deadpan humour. You made me realise how much I enjoy well-executed and articulated deadpan humour. The Coen Brothers have written it into Marge's character – continued moments of ironic delight (something of a labour of love, perhaps, for Joel Coen writing dialogue for his wife, Frances McDormand). They have also written it into their screenplay, the fidgety nervousness of William H. Macy's Jerry Lundergaard, hiring hitmen, edgy in dealing with his father-in-law, earnestly pleading for money, and getting more and more tangled. And there is irony and deadpan humour in the performances of Steve Buscemi and Peter Stormare as the hitmen, one designed for incessant conversation and the other with his lugubrious silences, clashes, taking time off with the prostitutes, the brutality of their violence and the deadpan of the aftermath. And even more deadpan in the disposal of the killers.

That is what I'm thinking now but, to make sure, I'm going back to some of the thoughts I wrote in my original review back in 1996.

'A film from the Coen Brothers. But trying to describe and review Fargo is not easy. It is difficult to categorise the movies made by the very clever Coen Brothers' (and that was written not knowing the great variety of their films in the coming two decades). 'They use the well-known American genres of thrillers, comedies, police investigations but turn them into movies that often puzzle the general audience but are critically well-received.'

It was one of the best films of 1996. A warning – it has some violent murders. But it puts this violence in the context of American society, of greed and crime, of hit men and guns as well as the mixture of human niceness, shrewdness and stupidity. Which means that we laugh one minute and are taken aback the next. So it is a funny, thoughtful, as well as a visceral, movie. William H. Macy is excellent as a dumb car salesman who gets the brainwave to hire killers to abduct his wife and demand a ransom to be paid by her wealthy father.

It doesn't quite work out that way. One, because he is stupid and nervous; two, because the killers are stupid and violent; and three, because we think at first that the very pregnant chief of police, Marge, is stupid, but. in her straightforward and honest way, she is definitely not. Her character dramatises the point that common-sense and decency are at the core of being human. The spoof of Scandinavian-American accents, vocabulary and manners is a sometimes hilarious Minnesota version of Harold Pinter.'

The Pinter reference comes as something of a surprise over twenty years later.

Actually, reading this again, I am quite pleased at how I responded back in 1996.

A summary thumbnail: complex and entertaining.

Dear *Monsieur Vincent*,

It's a very long time since I first saw you. You are one of the earliest films I saw, back in 1947 or 1948.

There are two things I want to write to you about. The first actually concerns subtitles. I think you must have been the first French film that I ever saw, but I cannot remember whether you were dubbed or whether there were subtitles. I have never had difficulties with subtitles so maybe you introduced to me to them with some ease. I remember that you screened at the small cinema, the Savoy, in Bligh Street, in Sydney, not right in the centre where the other theatres were but tucked away, on the way down to Circular Quay. It was where foreign language films were screened in Sydney.

The other thing is your portrait of St Vincent De Paul. As I look back, you must have been the first film I ever saw with the life of a saint on screen. Come to think of it, and I have been thinking about this quite hard, I don't remember seeing another film on the life of a saint until 1973, just over 25 years later, Francis of Assisi in *Brother Son, Sister Moon*. Sorry, just remembered *The Song of Bernadette*! In more recent years, especially with films made for television, there are quite a few more films about saints. But, back then...

Which means that my main cinema images of the life of a saint were from you. I wonder how much they shaped my ideas of what a saint was and was like during my primary and secondary years at school. I know we were urged to read popular lives of the saints, especially in primary school, my even having to read them over the microphone in the hall at OLSH Bowral before the screening started or, as frequently happened, we stopped after the first reel and Sister Philomena judged that the film was suitable for the elderly and retired sisters so we paused, listened to the stories, the sisters came over to the hall and we started all over again.

It also means that you were the main image of the ministry of a priest that I absorbed through films in those years. Soon there were Spencer Tracy and Bing Crosby but Pierre Fresnay as St Vincent De Paul was the first.

One thing to note is that you are in black and white. You are not a colour-processed biography of a saint. Nor were you romantic. As I remember, Vincent lived a very hard life. Whenever I see the galley scenes for Jean Valjean in the various versions of *Les Misérables*, my memory always goes back to seeing Vincent de Paul and his time in the galleys, almost two hundred years before Jean Valjean. So, it wasn't a surprise to see a suffering saint. Actually, the promotion of martyr saints in our consciousness was very strong in those days.

[Postscript: I now remember that we did see another priest film at primary school, *Guilty of Treason*, the story of the trial and persecution of Cardinal Mindzenty of Hungary – reinforcement of the martyr perspective.]

I remember that priesthood was important for Vincent. But I also remember some grim sequences of his working with the poor, the depictions of the poor in France at the time and his being among them. Which means that when I first heard of the Saint Vincent De Paul Society, it made a lot of sense because I had seen the saint with the poor.

In retrospect, I remember that Vincent was ministering during the reign of King Louis XIII, not always the most savoury period in French history – are you aware of the presentation of his court, or at least some effete aspects of his court, in Ken Russell's film of that same period, the period of Richelieu, *The Devils*? I remember wondering when I first saw *The Devils* how Vincent De Paul fitted into this atmosphere of politics, self-indulgence and madness. Certainly, a challenge.

I find it a bit embarrassing to look back also and find that I have no memory of Louise de Marillac and her collaboration with Vincent in establishing the Daughters of Charity. In a way, the archetype of saints in our consciousness was very much priestly, very much masculine. More's the pity.

So I wanted to acknowledge your presence in my life, in my cinema-going life, a very early presence – and providing me with great credibility about the church, the ministry of priests, self-sacrificing work for the poor, something of the reality of saints in the long Catholic history.

Dear *The Life and Death of Colonel Blimp*,

Because this letter to you will soon meander into reflections about Britain, Great or not, I thought I had better tell you at once that you are a film that I have admired long since.

I have read that Winston Churchill wanted, sight unseen, to have you banned in 1943, considering that you would be undermining British morale and patriotism during the war. That was a kind of Blimpish thing to do. Churchill had misunderstood or had been misinformed.

One of my first reactions when I first saw you in the 1970s was a certain, perhaps mean-minded, enjoyment of your satirical look at superior British self-confidence. I was not familiar with the cartoons of David Low, his barbs at pretentiousness, and military smugness with his Colonel Blimp, but it certainly seemed that writers-directors, Michael Powell and Emeric Pressburger, had been spurred on to a different kind of cinema war effort than might have been expected. It was not that they were not patriotic, we think of *49th Parallel, One of Our Aircraft is Missing* as well as *A Canterbury Tale*. They were taking on a fuddy-duddy military establishment that believed in a blend of a real and make-believe past, that could be detrimental to Britain's involvement in World War II, especially considering the impact of the Blitz and the Battle of Britain.

My point of view is very much that of Australian republicanism. In early 1954, we lined up outside St Vincent's Hospital, Darlinghurst, to wave to the young Queen Elizabeth as she drove past. That seemed to fulfil any longings for monarchy – although we did go and see the films that were made of her tour of the Pacific, New Zealand and Australia. Actually, at the end of that same month of February, all the schoolchildren on the South coast of New South

Wales as well as from the schools in the Southern Highlands, were assembled on an oval at Wollongong, en masse, to wave again to the Queen. Enough said, enough done. I went reviewing while Charles and Diana were married. I went to an IT tutorial when Diana was buried.

I first saw you in the 1970s. We were ready for your kind of anti-establishment criticism. We had seen Kubrick's critique of the French in World War I in *Paths of Glory*. But, in the 1960s, it was accepted, even the done thing, to enter into post Dr Strangelove satire on things military. Joan Littlewood upped the pace with *Oh What a Lovely War*. There was John Lennon in *How I Won the War*. Then, after *M*A*S*H*, open slather. Seeing you again after 45 years or so, given the 21st-century history of Britain, your themes are still pointed and relevant.

Roger Livesy brought the pomposity of Clive Candy immediately alive when he is astounded at the presumption of an early raid on the Turkish baths when 'the war begins at midnight', relying on past and gentlemanly codes of engaging in battle. But you show he was not always like that, taking us back to the period post-the Boer War, his challenging the Germans in the Kaiser years, his participation in World War I, searching out his old German friend, Theo, in the British POW camp, he and his friends offering support to the defeated enemy, an 'appeacement'.

But with his bafflement by the 1930s, by the rise of Hitler, his bellicose assumptions about war and his being banned to lecture like so on the BBC, we appreciate that, living in the past, he had become outmoded. Actually, he is saved by more down-to-earth war participation, The Home Guard (with John Laurie playing his aide, Murdoch, eventually marching into 80 episodes of televisions *Dad's Army*).

You treat us to changing attitudes and stances over a 40 year period, 1903-1943. But, even in the 1970s, let alone now, each of your three eras looks like history to us. I have to shake myself to appreciate that your opening and closing, 1943, was contemporary, modern, up-to-date, how Britain was fighting World War II. Audiences on your first release were seeing themselves as they were, clothes, band music, slang, cheeky attitudes... For the audiences of those days, the period of Colonel Blimp was over.

This change was powerfully dramatised by the three characters played by Deborah Kerr, the continuity of the English woman but, some extraordinary changes from 1903 to 1943. At first, we saw her as a strong-minded governess in Berlin, conscious of explicit anti-English antagonisms, a suffragette, something which Clive Candy could not understand or approve of. By 1918, she has gone on active service as a nurse, becomes a wife who could stand side-by-side with her husband, not dominated by him. And, by 1943, there she is a military driver, eagerly participating in the war games, down-to-earth, a modern woman.

While it is difficult to put oneself in the mind and sensibilities of the 1943 British audience, you are still a sometimes sly, sometimes cheekily ribbing, classic of British cinema, fine to look at with your striking colour photography, re-creating those different periods, Roger Livesy giving a tour-de-force performance as Clive Candy living through the different eras. Britannia used to rule – but, Britannia's time came and went.

Dear *Se7en*,

'Dear' is not the first greeting that comes to mind when writing to you. You have to be one of the grimmest serious films around, even up to the final moment with Morgan Freeman's Detective Somerset looking back over the events of your narrative, quoting Ernest Hemingway: 'the world is a fine place and worth fighting for' – and his stating that he agrees with the latter part of the quote, not the first part.

I remember seeing you in the mid-90s and being very struck by your exploration of the darkness of the human spirit. And director, David Fincher, keeps the whole film dark. We often are peering at the screen – and the detectives searching the obscured crime scenes with torches. Early in the 90s, in our Catholic international Cinema Organisation, there was quite some discussion about films like you, centring on Abel Ferrara's *Bad Lieutenant*, films about the human spirit that echoed Psalm 130 and its cry to God, 'out of the depths'. In fact, in 1999, Pope John Paul II in an address urged this kind of exploration of the dark heart, the reality of evil in our world, in our lives.

But I would add, in your regard, another phrase that emerged not long after, in the wake of a realisation that there are some cries from the depths that seem not to be heard – or there are some characters who refuse to cry from the depths, opt for the darkness in their hearts. Gaspar Noe directed a film around 2008, *Enter the Void*, which seemed to me to give voice, or a title, to films like yourself where there seems to be no escape, or as in Sartre's title, *No Exit*, narratives that seemed devoid of hope.

What attracted you to me initially was your presentation of two detectives, serious men, investigating what must be called a gruesome case (or, at some moments, beyond gruesome). I will confess to being an avid reader of crime fiction, with quite a list of favourite authors and admired detectives (on both sides of the Atlantic). Most of the authors have quite a way with words, an ability to create unexpected and often humorous metaphors and similes which make the steps of character development, the following of clues, the unmasking of criminals, both entertaining and satisfying.

This is not quite the case with your two detectives, the serious loner, about to retire, William Somerset, yet another fine screen presence by Morgan Freeman (and his extraordinary deeply telling voice), and ambitious rookie, David Mills, a young Brad Pitt, here a bit prone to over-heated acting.

On that level, you are well worth seeing, the interactions between the two men, the resigned loneliness of the older man who was born to detect and becomes more and more involved in the case, clashing with the young man, trying to guide him, exasperated at his foolhardiness, seeming to listen and then doing the opposite of the advice (even tragically at your end). So, you are not a buddy movie in the expected sense, but an exploration of professional collaboration which does not always succeed.

Your screenplay is effective in introducing the character of Mills' wife, Tracy (a sympathetic Gwyneth Paltrow), who has found the move to the city very difficult, the apartment being shaken often by the passing subway train, her being pregnant, unable to tell her husband but able to confide and get sound advice from Somerset. And, at the closing of the film, because of these sequences, the pathos and grief are intense. I seem to be delaying on the detectives when, of course, your title (with the tantalising substitution of the V by 7) indicates that I should be concentrating on the crimes and the criminal. You give a hint, more than a hint, during the complex collage of the opening credits, something manic and sinister. With the titles of gluttony and greed for the first two victims, we are introduced into the complexities of good and evil in this world, the evil symbolised by the old tradition, incorporated into Christianity, of The Seven Deadly Sins.

This means that you draw us into morality and immorality in our world, a blogger using the phrase 'culpability of the culture', taking us into the depths. The criminal, ironically called John Doe, usually the name for unknown victims, is madness with a mission. Kevin Spacey is superbly sinister (the same year as he won an Oscar for yet another intrinsically evil character, Verbal/ Keyser Soze, in *The Usual Suspects*). As the two detectives explore some of the depths of the deadly sins, going back to Dante, to Chaucer, to Thomas Aquinas, we are reminded of the evil that the sins indicate. But, with the close-up detail, probably excessive for some audience sensitivities, we have to face up to the consequences of the sins in our world.

But especially towards your end, as the criminal unmasks himself and offers a final challenge to the detectives, diabolical in intent and in execution, you make explicit that he sees himself as a moralising preacher, to rid the world of evil, speeches against his victims he has condemned to torture and death, no appreciation of human frailty, no mercy. We can see him as an avenging-God figure, as a hellish Satan-figure.

The saddest thing is that as an image of God, he is diabolical. If this is God, no wonder God is denied. In fact, your story and the ending can be seen as a plea for some kind of forgiveness, some kind of mercy, the redemptive image of God and Jesus in our world. But, with that Hemingway quote, the appeal is to nobility in human nature in a Godless world which strives to make the world a better place – even if, as in your story, this might seem impossible.

By the end, you are a challenging, seemingly unrelenting, contemporary morality play.

Dear *A Star is Born*,

I'm really pleased to be writing to you. It seems strange, looking back, that you were such an important film for me when I was young – even stranger when I realise that, seeing you in 1954, I was 14 turning 15. At school, we did have a number of films with adult themes, but liking you at that age seems a touch precocious. However, that's what it was.

And the version we saw at that time was considerably cut, almost thirty minutes we have been told. The pleasure recently was to see the restored version, the best part of three hours, sequences reintroduced and, where the original was lost, photo substitution – rather a lot, it seemed, in the first part of the film. But there was great pleasure in seeing you again. There was your story, there was the presence of Judy Garland, performing and singing at her peak, one of the best of James Mason's performances.

It may seem strange but the word that suggests itself about your impact is that your story is 'archetypal': it is a rising and dying story, or a dying and rising story – told many a time but given some biblical significance in the story of John the Baptist, his being the precursor of Jesus, his successful ministry at the Jordan, recognising Jesus and baptising him, Jesus praising him as the 'greatest born of woman' but then adding that any of his disciples was greater than John. John himself said I must decrease, he must increase. That is something of the archetypal pattern for your story.

And except – for some reason – not in the 1990s, there was a movie version of you every twenty years, the 1930s, 1950s, 1970s, and 2018. There was, of course, the initial film of 1932, *What Price Hollywood?* (Never seen it but the comment is that it is pre-code and rather racy), directed by your director, George Cukor, which set the story going on screen. But you set the musical precedent as George Cukor returns to direct..

As I think back, you would be one of the first films I saw which opened up narratives of collapse, self-loathing, alcoholism (which was not new for me, with alcoholic neighbours each side of us and at the back of our home in Woollahra), despair and suicide. Strong stuff for a 14-year-old. As I watched you again, I was moved as James Mason decided that he should disappear from his wife's life, seeing him go down to the beach, walking into the sea.

But I want to tell you a humorous anecdote. It illustrates how naive a 14-year-old can be. I remember at the time thinking it was absolutely hilarious when Esther Blodgett went to get her first pay cheque and lined up for her salary at booth for the letter B – but her name had been changed to Vicki Lester and the man at the booth said to her 'go to L'. That seemed to be daring at the time – go to hell!! Well, on watching you the other week, that scene came and went without any fanfare, and I couldn't believe that I had remembered it, a humorous reminiscence, for sixty-five years!

For many of us, the impact of a movie belongs very much to the times in which we saw it. This is particularly the case for me watching you again, remembering again. Just thinking of Judy Garland, fifteen years on from *The Wizard of Oz* (and only 14 years to go until her death), her screen presence, her singing, the possibilities with you in 1954, the disappointment of her not getting the Oscar, and only three more screen performances to go. But she did have success with concerts and touring (and seeing *Judy* recently, with Renee Zellweger bringing her alive, looking, sounding, performing just like Judy as Esther Blodgett was a moving experience).

So, Judy Garland, a star of her times. Twenty years on, there is Barbra Streisand, a star of her times. Then, more than forty years on, the impact of Lady Gaga and acclamation for her performance. Images of different kinds of stardom. And, of course, different styles of singing. Judy Garland came from the MGM musicals, the melodies of the 1930s and 40s, and many of them reprised wonderfully in the long episode of *Born in a Trunk*, let alone impact of *The Man that Got Away*. By the 70s, Barbra Streisand's virtuosity combined the trends of the 1960s and 70s, although she won an Oscar for her composition of *Evergreen* (saying in her acceptance speech that never in her wildest dreams had she thought of this – except, perhaps, every night's wildest dreams!). In our times now, Lady Gaga can belt out songs but, of course, there was the Oscar-winning *Shallow*.

And reflecting the times, Esther Blodgett became a movie star, and the songs were staged on movie sets, audiences responding to the movies. With Barbra Streisand, it was out to concerts and crowds. And concerts and performance are what is to the fore with Lady Gaga and Bradley Cooper, the songs filmed at and during actual concerts.

So recently, you have given me the opportunity to be nostalgic, going back six decades, living in the past, reliving the past, remembering the initial impact, appreciating how much I absorbed when young, in those days which seem now rather safe and comfortable, and my realising how much I was formed by those times, by you and those movies of those times.

Dear *Scott of the Antarctic*,

You may be well surprised to receive a letter from me. In fact, I'm rather surprised that I'm writing it. I first saw you back in the late 1940s at school, and was very impressed – as we were at that time, more knowledgeable and familiar with British history rather than with our own Australian history, let alone pre-1788 culture and history, proud of the British heritage even if our personal heritage was Irish, particularly so in the years following the end of World War II. Perhaps more of that later.

The reason for writing to you is that you came to mind quite vividly yesterday while I was watching the 2020 science-fiction thriller, *Underwater*. If no one can hear you scream in space, what about deep down on the ocean floor, six miles and more down in the Mariana Trench? *Underwater* was well made, a B-budget story (a 'monsters of the deep' variation), with A-budget technology. So the question of why you came to mind. And, when remembering John Mills as Captain Robert Scott, memories of Mills' role in the submarine drama, *Morning Departure*, heroism in the face of inevitable death when trapped underwater, also came to mind.

The challenge to an audience of *Underwater* or, even of yourself, is: why would we put ourselves in such a situation? And, if we were, challenged to stay put and die, accepting our fate, or make every effort to find an exit from impending death, what would we choose? The other question which arose is what would we do if we found we were hindering the safety and progress of the others? Would we make ourselves a sacrifice, dying that others would live? This is certainly the case with *Underwater* and its personal dilemmas.

But up came the memory of Scott's Antarctic expedition, the heroism, seeming futility, explorers trapped by nature as well as their own decisions. And vividly returned that memory of Oates saying to the other members of the expedition, 'I'm just going outside. I may be some time'.

I was 11 or 12 when I first saw you and experienced that sequence – and it has always remained with me – self-sacrifice presented in the noblest kind of way, Oates actually killing himself. Because the sequence has remained your most vivid in my memory over the decades, I realised how influenced we can be by drama, by the stories we see up there on the screen, shaping our attitudes, perhaps for life. And combined with this memory of Oates' sacrifice, the stories of the Christian martyrs we constantly heard and even relished, which were also shaping our Catholic perspectives during those years.

I have just been looking up the *Internet Movie Database* to check how bloggers have responded to you. Some go back to the atmosphere in 1948 – Scott and his fellows as heroic British explorers, the honour of Great Britain, stiff upper lip attitudes towards disaster, then again, the challenge to stiff upper lip as the expedition failed and the way that the explorers interacted with each other. Oates' minimalist statement as he made his decision to give his life is the epitome of reticent stiff upper lip. This was British movie heroism 1940s style, war and post-war.

Of course, there has been a lot of revisionist history after the expedition's failure and challenging the details of the film. While we liked and honoured heroes and icons in those days, praising heroic virtue, bypassing or ignoring personal flaws, poor strategic decisions, incompetencies in management, even statues on pedestals in these times are more often seen to have feet of clay.

When you first came out, we knew more about Scott and dramatised his heroism than we did about the Norwegian who actually reached the South Pole first, Roald Amundsen. We might have heard of Ernest Shackleton. And we knew less about our own Australian Antarctic explorer, Douglas Mawson.

So, a tribute to your heroic ambitions, the strong British cast in their performances, the striking colour photography. But that was then, this is now. We re-appraise everything and everyone. But as I sat watching *Underwater* and the moral dilemmas faced by the group trying to find a way to reach the surface, menaced by horrendous monsters of tentacles and teeth, the moral issue of sacrificing oneself so that others could survive, seemed so important both emotionally and intellectually.

Dear *Mary and Max*,

You are one of my favourite Australian films. I'm taking the opportunity to think aloud about why this is the case.

Of course, the most immediate impact is in your animation, the skill of Adam Elliot (after his Oscar for the short film, *Harvey Crumpet* – and the continuing wish that he would make another film), the idiosyncratic drawing of his characters, the dingy landscapes of suburban Melbourne in the 1970s and 1980s, the black-and-white skyline of New York City. Another word for those idiosyncratic characters, grotesques. This is a word association with Fellini's films, performers who looked grotesque in real life, bringing a challenging as well as an alarming range of characters. The characters are, physically, all out of proportion, small and eccentric bodies (with Max as obese), large heads. But, with the voice talent, the characters are alive and communicate themselves as real.

Which means that there is a whole lot of caricature going on. Mary's mother, Vera, with her dangling cigarette, her fondness for sherry (explaining the predilection for 'cups of tea'), saying she was borrowing when actually she was shoplifting, is the extreme caricature, no sympathy for her. Norm, Mary's father, is practically invisible, putting tabs on the products in the factory, retreating to work in the back shed. So what is Elliot saying about the Australian family?

One answer is that it is parody. We appreciate the reality as we grimace at life, grimace at and with this portrait of life at Mount Waverley.

It is something the same with the portrait of Max. He is a caricature, a 44-year-old man living alone, with pet fish, obese, apostle for chocolate hotdogs. But, the caricature elicits some sympathy, moments of compassion, when he explains to us that he suffers from Aspergers – and obesity.

Which means then that you are a tale of aloneness, of isolation, loneliness, very sad aspects of the human condition. Which also means that your narrative comes alive when young Mary, with all kinds of questions, especially where babies come from (and her gawkiness and glasses!), decides to send a letter to a random address from the phone book, in New York City.

Mary and Max come to more vivid life as we listen to their letters, Mary and her questions, recommending sweetened condensed milk, posting chocolates, and Max sitting at his typewriter, describing the different jobs that he has had, his attendance at help meetings, the advice of his counsellor, communication over the years – and Mary's later discovery that he had kept every letter, laminated each letter covering the walls of his apartment with the joy of their correspondence.

Adam Elliot wrote the screenplay but the voice-over is narration by Barry Humphries, a delight to listen to, more in his Sandy Stone vein, quiet reminiscences, and attention to domestic details, but not without some verbal barbs in the Dame Edna waspishness. I found the correspondence between them and the images and narrative always stirring.

But you are also very sad. Mary's life at home is sad. Her growing up is sad. There is a glimmer of hope with her falling in love with Damian across the street. But I still wonder what Elliot was getting at about Australian males, love and marriage, when he reveals that Damian is gay and goes to live with his sheep farmer friend in New Zealand.

Mary seems to have some hope when she goes to the University and studies Aspergers, publishes a book and eagerly sends it to Max who interprets it so badly, so hurt, sending the M from his typewriter to her – but you are not without hope, Mary and Max both in the depths but finding ways to say that they are sorry. Reconciliation is certainly possible. And the pathos of Mary, going to New York, finding Max dead, seeing the laminated letters, realising that, despite the sadness, there had been joy in friendship, breaking through loneliness, in both of their lives.

I would like to add that the marvellous voicing, Bethany Whitmore and then Tony Collette as Mary, Philip Seymour Hoffman Max, Eric Bana as Damian, a great number of supporting voice cast all excellent. And I would like to add a comment about the musical score, the continued delight of all kinds of melodies and songs emerging, sometimes snippets, sometimes commentary on the action – from Prokofiev and *Romeo and Juliet* to Puccini and the humming song, from *Zorba the Greek* to *Que Sera. Sera*, the joy of the Typewriting song, *That's Life* – and the cheery tones of Bert Kamfert, *That Happy Feeling* and *Swingin' Safari*. A wonderful commentary on the action in melody and song.

This letter can't do justice to the wonderful ingredients that make you a classic Australian film, classic animation, especially for adults, and a thought-provoker about what it is to be Australian (as well as an isolated New Yorker).

Dear *The Good, The Bad, and The Ugly*,

A great title for a Western. And a great title for a moral fable. And, immortalised in that initial whistle in Ennio Morricone's title theme, played with so many variations of instrument and pace throughout your long running time. There is always an exhilaration in hearing Morricone's theme.

And the reason for writing to you? It is really an opportunity for me to sort out something of what a Western film is. There is the 50 years and more tradition of what it was up there on the American screen up to the 1950s. A lot of cowboys and Indians, range wars and settlers, the cavalry. Then there is what happened with the unexpected phenomenon of the Spaghetti Western, especially in the 1960s. There is the up-and-down history of the Western since the 1970s, popularity, less popularity, revisionist consideration of what a Western really should be.

You had a great deal to contribute to this changing perspective on the Western. And thanks to Sergio Leone for his major contribution (not underestimating the other writers and directors of Spaghetti Westerns, many classics, many derivative imitations). I was surprised to be reminded that Leone began his writing career and what might now be described as spaghetti historical actioners, delving back into Roman history... But then came *The Man with No Name* (making Clint Eastwood much more than a name), the archetypal Spaghetti Westerns, *A Fistful of Dollars*, *For a Few Dollars More*. And then you, the climax of the trilogy, the vast look at the American West, the Hispanic territories in the South, and an immersion in aspects of the Civil War.

When I was growing up, the Westerns were very much about Cowboys and Indians, Cowboys versus Indians, the cavalry saving the day (for the cowboys), action shows but with a greater number of directors shaping what the Western would be in our consciousness, acknowledgment of John Ford. I'm very glad that I can remember the breakthrough with *Broken Arrow*, a shift in emphasis in looking at the Native Americans, not just as Hostiles (as they so often were towards the cavalierly hostile settlers moving west) but as men and women with human dignity, to be looked at with new eyes, with respect, with hope for some kind of peacemaking, reconciliation and atonement. *Broken Arrow* was released in 1950. In this, there were some examinations of conscience about white and red hostilities, and in 1971 the story of *Little Big Man*.

The Spaghetti Westerns, like yourself, did not focus so much on the Indians. You created stories about gunslingers, the law, outlaws, greed, bounty hunters, the survival of the remote towns, vengeance and violence.

On the one hand, your schematic title and schematic interactions between the good, a rather silent poncho-wearing Clint Eastwood, the bad, the sly and avaricious Lee Van Cleef, the comic opportunist, crafty and slippery, providing a mixture of the comic and the sinister, in Eli Wallach's Tuko, the ugly, with a commendation to him because it is he who has the most complex acting task and performance. You use all kinds of conventions to illustrate the nature of each of these men, there are exercises of power over each other, Eastwood dragged mercilessly through the desert by Wallach, then tables turning. Lee Van Cleef and his relentless violence is actually and symbolically bad. And, schematically, you have them confront each other in the cemetery, death to the bad, torment to the ugly as he thinks he is being hanged, and nonchalant survival for the good.

So, in a sense, you are an archetype of this kind of Western – continually enhanced by Morricone's theme, by the plaintiff chant of the prisoners of war, of the climactic, dramatic music there in the cemetery.

But what also impressed me and has stayed with me is your picture of the Civil War, the settings in the South, the invasion by the Union military, the rounding up of enemy soldiers, the prisoner of war camps, the doctors and their trying to help the wounded, with the peaceful sequence of Eastwood comforting a dying soldier, bringing some kind of heart to so much of the seemingly heartless action.

You and the Spaghetti Westerns were very important in the 1960s, a perspective on the American West from Europe, filming in Spain, a re-creation of the American West but also a reinterpretation, and always with an eye on the moral issues, on Western heroism, on the sometimes stupidity of the ugly, the malice of the bad, and the ambiguous virtue of the good.

Dear *Hereafter*,

I am surprised. Here I am writing to another Clint Eastwood film. But you are also a Peter Morgan film. His credentials are impressive. But he was best known for his political dramas like *The Queen*, *The Special Relationship*, *The Last King of Scotland* and *Frost/Nixon*. Then he went and wrote the vast television series, *The Crown*. However, he has gone in a very different direction this time, a more meditative approach to his storytelling.

You are an impressive film for audiences who like to reflect on the themes of their movies.

I found it very interesting that Clint Eastwood should choose to direct you – and you were in production when he turned 80 in May 2010. You are striking movie-making by an old man who is in control of his skills but is thinking thoughts beyond this world. He is exploring themes of near-death experience, the possibilities of an afterlife and of communicating with those who have died.

Clint Eastwood had been directing for over 40 years (and still working at 90 plus!) as well as developing a screen persona for longer: an iconic western figure in the Spaghetti Westerns, the *Dirty Harry* policeman in that series as well as the symbolic gunfighters in his 'religious' westerns. He brought this thematic acting career to a head with the wonderful (and redemptive) *Gran Torino* (but supplemented it a decade later with *The Mule*). He also took a greater interest in religious themes, explicitly Catholic, in *Million Dollar Baby* and, a lesson for young clergy, in *Gran Torino*.

Your opening sequence is quite overwhelming, action before the reflection. Your re-creation of the tsunami in Thailand received an Oscar nomination. We were in it. We were swept along, unable to control anything, with the vast and swift-moving waves, relentless. But you settle down to tell three very different stories. Your structure is quite schematic. Sections of each story are told in regular turn until, in a pleasing way, the three central characters are brought together in London.

It should be said that you seem to have quite a European feel rather than a glossy Hollywood style. That and your serious subject of the hereafter might account for your not doing very well at the US box-office.

In fact, we are in Europe for your first story, set in Paris. We share the memory of a vivacious television journalist and host (Cecile de France) who tries to come to terms with what she experienced in almost drowning in the tsunami. It affects her relationships, her work and sends her to Switzerland to consult an expert on near-death (Marthe Keller).

Then to the US for your second story, set in San Francisco. Matt Damon is George working in a factory. We learn that he has powers, mysterious to him as well as to others, whereby he knows matters about a person by touching them. He regrets these powers and the effect they have had on his life and resists the attempts of his brother (Jay Mohr) to make a business out of the phenomenon. There is an episode where a young woman (Bryce Dallas Howard) who does a cooking course with George and finds out more than she anticipated or wanted.

Back to Europe for your third story, this time set in London. Twins live with their addict mother, trying to shield her from social workers. When one of the twins is killed in an accident and the other is sent to foster care, he wants to know more about his brother whom he senses is always with him. Frankie and George McLaren play the twins as recognisably ordinary boys.

It might seem impossible for the three central characters to meet but they do, not in an overtly contrived way, but satisfyingly. George's love for Charles Dickens' novels is an important factor. He listens to tapes of the novels (read by Derek Jacobi whom he meets at the London Book Fair).

Clint Eastwood shows great sensitivity in dealing with the themes and in the performances he gets from your central figures.

You are a film to surrender to and searching audiences will find you richly rewarding.

Dear *La Belle Epoque*,

Just back home from seeing you. I had better first give you the context for writing to you.

We were at the media preview of the 2020 French Film Festival, drinks and nibbles to get us in a proper French frame of mind, a speech by the director in charge of selecting the program, enthusiasm for the films to be screened, the Melbourne media definitely on side. He explained that you received a seven-minute standing ovation at the 2019 Cannes Film Festival: Oh yes, mais oui, très françois...

As it turned out, we really enjoyed watching you, a lot of Gallic humour, an inventive screenplay, ultimately, quite a lot to think about. So, here I am.

After the final credits, my friends Sharon and Pete were enthusiastic. Since you had your central character travelling imaginatively back to a year that he chose, 1974, when he first met his wife – though now he is depressed and she disappointed. Pete was so in tune with the many songs of the time that it was obviously a period he identified with. And then he asked me: where would I go back to. Of course, he suggested to the time of Jesus! However, I was immediately conscious that I had had a happy and fruitful life (at least up to this stage, age 80) and that I did not have a year that I would go back to rediscover what I might have missed and lost.

And then it struck me. I would go back to 1957, my first year of training in my religious congregation, my novitiate year.

Before I say more, I would like to get myself more context from your imaginative screenplay. After we have been introduced to your central couple, Victor and Marianne, great French veterans Daniel Auteuil and Fanny Ardant, we find that their son has a friend who has created something of a mini-industry. He has studios. He has equipment. He employs a vast number of actors. And he has clients who choose to participate in a re-enactment of the period that they choose, especially in their own life. They are conscious of what is happening and join in the drama which is based on suggestions and information they have given. It is somewhat reminiscent of *The Truman Show*, with the director 'playing God', intervening, directing the action, trying to be both factual and creative. The cast study their roles and perform with some zest and accuracy. I suppose it is something like *The Truman Show* in reverse. Truman was directed, unknowingly, and was discovering his life as he lived it. He needed to discover a newer and freer life.

So, back to 1957. Off we went to a novitiate in the New South Wales countryside, away from everyone. There is a complaint that we were all too young in those days but, in fact, we had to make decisions in our final years of school as to what we might do with our lives. It is not that we were too young; it was that we were quite inexperienced. We were not at all worldly-wise. And, over the years, as we did become more experienced and wise (we hope), there is a great deal of regret that this kind of experience and wisdom was not part of our novitiate formation. There really wasn't much scope.

Our novice master, Father Butler, was a very strict/austere man. He believed in a prevailing spirituality of the time, that we became true to ourselves by humility (and a lot of humiliations which seemed somewhat absurd at the time and even more absurd as the years pass). Our wills had to be broken so that we would submit to God's will (which, later, some of us realised, was just the whim of the superior). This was harsh experience, accepted and somewhat taken for granted at the time by us, but having some detrimental effects on us all, in very different ways.

I don't know whether you are familiar with the American film, *An Officer and a Gentleman*, remembered romantically by many, a film of military training with Louis Gossett Jr (he must have acted well because he got an Oscar for this performance) as a harsh, sometimes sadistic, relentless imposer of military discipline and beyond, the breaking of the will. I should tell you that I saw this on the 25th anniversary of my first taking of vows – and, I'm afraid, I did not find it romantic at all. I was down there in the mud, doing pushups with a humiliated Richard Gere – no desire to see it again.

In succeeding years, many of us had wonderful opportunities to become more spiritually worldly-wise, able to understand and appreciate our chosen way of life, our authentic heart spirituality, make it a motivation for our ministry. For many, this discovery made for perseverance. For many others, there were moments of disappointment, better self-awareness, and moments of disillusionment, departure.

I have no regrets but thinking about you all the way home in the two trams, I decided I would write to you, a compliment to your director, Nicolas Bedos (born only in 1980!) and his insights, inviting his audiences to go back – and, with great hope, rediscover original zest, love, commitment.

Dear *Sorry We Missed You*,

Perhaps it is sufficient to say that you are a Ken Loach film. And to add, you are a very fine Ken Loach film (directed when he was in his early 80s). Some have noted that you may be his last.

Ken Loach has immersed his audiences for over 50 years in the life of working-class Britons, mostly in England, sometimes in Scotland, occasionally in the United States and Latin America. He has certainly been the champion of the working class from films, almost documentary-like, *Cathy Come Home* and *Kes* in the 1960s and, finding a consistent pace in the early 1990s, a striking film almost every two years, winning the Palme D'Or in Cannes twice, for his Irish Civil War drama, *The Wind That Shakes the Barley* and then for *I, Daniel Blake*. I would like to add that he has won the most awards for any director from Catholic and Ecumenical juries around the world.

Which is a cue for me to add two anecdotes. When SIGNIS celebrated the 30th anniversary of the Ecumenical Award in Cannes, a collaboration between Catholics and Protestants, Loach was invited to a special function, medal award, for his being our most honoured director. There was a strike at the time by workers in the equivalent of the industrial union for entertainment workers. He met two of the young strikers outside and brought them in to illustrate his acceptance speech. Typical Loach! The other anecdote goes way back, to 1969, to outback Broken Hill in New South Wales, a media seminar with Sisters of Mercy. Those were the days in which we are discussing the new wave of more serious and challenging films. It never rains in Broken Hill but it sprinkled that night at the drive-in, the Sisters using windscreen wipers, battery flat by the end of the film. The genial worker at the drive-in asked about the films, especially *Poor Cow*, which is

Loach's earliest feature film, remarking that it was 'a bit rough'. 'Oh', exclaimed the superior, 'that's what we came for'!

Tribute should also be given to your writer, Paul Laverty, who has written all the screenplays for Loach's film since 1996. (Laverty trained to be a priest at the Scots College in Rome for several years, did not continue but has had what one might call a social justice ministry in writing the screenplays for the Loach films – Loach told us that he discovered through Laverty that the Catholic Church was not a monolith).

This time you show us details of Newcastle-upon-Tyne, symbolic of all those northern Loach locations, introduced to Ricky Turner (Kris Hitchen), a driver, anxious to make ends meet, to buy a home for his family instead of renting, who becomes part of the franchise of seemingly-independent drivers in a highly organised co-op for parcel delivery. While it sounds good, he has to buy his own van, sell his wife's car to cover the deposit, submit himself to a highly demanding regime, timetable, supervision, regulations that require him to find substitute drivers if he has family troubles – and there are plenty with his 16-year-old son, Seb (Rhys Stone), who is skipping school, painting graffiti, sullen at home. His wife, Abbie (Debbie Honeywood), is admirable, a home carer who is wonderful with the elderly. There is also a young daughter at home.

Pure Laverty, one might say, pure Loach. And focusing our social concern on the now, some of the dire consequences on workers of the Global Financial Crisis. There is a Loach continuity for over fifty years.

In your early sequences, we have a marvellous opportunity to see a wide range of those in need, men and women, their gratitudes and ingratitudes, personal idiosyncrasies, the range of ordinary human nature. We travel in the van, encounter all kinds of people receiving their packages, some gruff, some genial, some demanding... We also travel in the bus with Abbie, encountering quite a number of home shut-ins who require patient attention, feeding, cleaning...

I really appreciated one joyous day when the daughter accompanies her father delivering the parcels, even a kindly lady giving her some change to buy some lollies. But Ricky is then informed that this is against the rules and someone has complained. In fact, the rules become more and more severe, relentless, the demanding letter of the law. The company boss calls himself the patron of 'nasty bastards' (not wrong) and has an extremely tin ear for any appeals for compassion over his unyielding regime rules.

Your narrative builds to some moments of high tension, Seb suspended and arrested for shoplifting, Ricky assaulted on the road, battered ... and, with the demanding timetable offering no minutes for toilet breaks, his urine bottle smashes and spreads over him. Abbie becoming more desperate, loving her husband and trying to mediate in the family. testing limits.

Loach and Laverty tell their story, straightforwardly but with higher dramatic tension in day-to-day lives, inviting the audience to share the life of the family, experience the problems, share the desperation.

You offer no resolution ending to speak of, the anxious family trying to argue Rick out of his own desperation, Rick sinking in debt because of missed calls, an expensive scanner broken. In pain from the bashing, experiencing his own internal anguish, blood clots and bruises, bruise-stained, he gets into the driving seat of the van, literally grim-faced, driving off in determination...

To where? (That would be symbolic if you are Loach's last film and this is final scene.)

Dear *A Matter of Life and Death*,

SBS World Movies channel, a wonderful collection of all kinds of films, is a great boon at the best of times and something of a solace in times of Covid-19. In recent months, they have been screening a number of films by The Archers, Michael Powell and Emeric Pressburger, their classics from the 1940s including *Colonel Blimp*, *Black Narcissus* (*Dear Movies* recipients). You were amongst their collection but I had seen you, probably in the 1970s, perhaps the 1980s, and had written a review with discussion questions at the time. Just checking on it again, I find that I had enjoyed watching you, been very impressed, noted the key themes even using the word 'rhetorical' about some scenes and the dialogue.

But the reason for watching you again was a great admiration felt for you by my friend and film reviewer, Alan Frank. For over twenty years, and again just recently, he referred to his watching you every year, obviously very, very high on his most admired list, and, as always, he quoted his favourite line – about Heaven – spoken by Marius Goring, 'one is starved of Technicolour up there'. All your sequences in the afterlife are in black and white, while all the sequences on Earth are in colour and he is exhilarated to come down and walk amongst beautifully red Technicoloured flowers.

As I watched you again, yesterday afternoon in Coronavirus lockdown, I realised that you were a film of wisdom, perhaps better appreciated by age and experience. Not that you didn't make an impact in your time and, if you care to check the *Internet Movie Database*, there is almost complete admiration, putting you on a pedestal as one of the best films ever, certainly one of the best British films ever.

So, what was it like watching you again?

First of all, I was very conscious of the date of the action, 2 May 1945. In fact, tomorrow week will be 2 May 2020, and a week later it will be VE Day, the 75th anniversary of the end of World War II in Europe. That was your setting. In the decades after, especially those immediately after the war, we were steeped in the British war films, including those of The Archers often sardonic in critique of British war tradition, but also, ultimately, war morale-boosting. Here is David Niven as Peter Carter, the seemingly doomed pilot, plane destroyed, no parachute, consoled by his radio contact with Kim Hunter's American June, ready to go to his death. But, surviving.

Your title, as well as the vast cosmic opening, gazing through the universe, finally finding Earth, meant that you had intentions of transcendence in your screenplay. Life and Death. With your scenes in your 'Heaven', there was a humane exploration, both serious and comic, of the possibilities of an afterlife (even when your three central characters, while on Earth, express uncertainty as to their belief in an afterlife). As some of the bloggers have noted, they would have, and I would have, liked even more imagination and speculation about death and the afterlife.

It seems to me that one of our problems these days is that, probably since *Star Wars*, there have been all kinds of fantasy explorations of the universe, alternate worlds, parallel universes, super heroic lives and deaths. And, as well, there has been such a spate of horror films, some elegant, some small-budget trash, all proposing 'supernatural' interventions of good and evil (generally evil) that we have rather conglomerate notions of life after death. Your seriously comic charm seems pleasingly ingenuous in retrospect.

But you offer us some delightful fantasy, the heavenly gatekeepers making some errors allowing Peter Carter twenty more hours on earth, enabling him to fall in love, to be treated with kindly empathy by a doctor, old Colonel Blimp himself, Roger Livesey, allowing audiences of sceptical disposition to have an opinion that it is all happening in Peter Carter's mind. But many (most?) audiences will be prepared to accept your benign consequences of death, the angels checking incomers, the selection of wings, the groups of various nationalities turning up (and some American GIs).

In fact, in retrospect, your attitude towards the United States and Americans is quite intriguing. Then I read a note that The Archers were asked by the Ministry of Defence to make a film that would promote post-war collaboration with the Americans. I presume the Ministry of Defence personnel were not anticipating what you actually produced for them, the trial of Peter Carter to justify his benefiting by the mistake of his surviving and receiving a longer lease on life.

In the heavenly court, hundreds of observers in attendance, most in some kind of uniform, nurses, Puritans from the past, Armed Forces, the prosecution against Carter is in Raymond Massey's rhetorical 18th century style critique of Britain (including his playing the commentary on a cricket match which is incomprehensible to him), matched by Roger Livesy for the defence playing some contemporary American music – at which both shudder. So, in retrospect, the War of Independence, the growth of the US, the continuance of the British supremacy even to Empire.

And this is reinforced by the members of the jury, quite a range of nationalities, reminding audiences of the extent of colonial dominance (as well as an Irishman with memories of British oppression). The judge, very British, agrees to a change of membership of the jury, all Americans. And here in 1946 is a reminder, very positively, of the range of backgrounds, ethnic contributions to the US. And though some have been glimpsed amongst the GIs, an African-American member of the jury. (It is interesting in retrospect to note that there are no women on the jury although some of the proceedings have been presided over by a woman.)

So you take us back into the past with some illumination of the past, British morale boosting, US support, but not without questions and critique, much of which has come to pass.

Some realism, entertaining and intriguing flights of fancy, fantasy, witty dialogue, literate references, the intrigue of black-and-white photography and the imagination of the afterlife, and our technicoloured earth. And one of the final morals of your story – the prosecutor emphasising the inexorable laws of the universe with the defence reminding the court and all of us, the all-important priority of love.

Dear *Fantasia*,

In retrospect, I am indebted to you. The retrospect in question is that of music education for those at school. My point is that at primary and secondary school, I was not introduced to the world of music – except for some years of learning the piano, which did give me some practical knowledge and experience, but our teacher became pregnant and we students had to give up our course. That sounds a little self-pitying but, in a sense, I do have self-pity because I still feel somewhat deprived, rather ignorant but, somehow or other, an innate drive to want to appreciate more.

But I was not absolutely bereft. While young, still at primary school, we went to see you at the Savoy in Bligh Street, Sydney, the small cinema where foreign language films were screened. Memory tells me that you were a delight, opening up another world, an easy visual introduction to the world of music. I have seen you several times since and continually delight in you.

In fact, as I write to you, your episodes are alive in my visual memory. And, although more limited, some of the melodies are alive in my musical memory as well. I thought I might name some of them as I write to you and enjoy a little visual and musical indulgence.

I'm remembering the visuals of the conductor, Leopold Stokowski, entering the stage, meeting his orchestra, raising his baton, 'let the performance begin'. I don't remember anything of Deems Taylor introducing each segment, but he obviously was an initial guide. Actually, I can't remember which piece was played first. Apart from Mickey Mouse (more later of Mickey), my initial memories are always of Tchaikovsky, the excerpts from *The Nutcracker Suite*. An easy classic, some people might say, but a pleasing introduction, and so many of the melodies have become familiar. But, of course, in the *Fantasia* world, the accompanying images are important. Just now I am seeing the water swirl of the *Waltz of the Flowers*, the 3/4 time rhythm (that comes from the theory that I studied for the music exams – which I did pass up to fourth-grade!). And now, the colours and shapes for the *Dance of the Sugar Plum Fairies*. The dancing mushrooms and their caps did look rather authentic for the *Chinese Dance*. I read that an Arabian dancer was the model for the shimmering goldfish for the *Arab Dance*. I have enjoyed recalling all this, *Nutcracker* forever!

While you were, originally, a musical fantasy for an adult audience (and honoured with awards accordingly), you were a Disney creation, always with an outreach to the child or the child within the adult. Mickey Mouse was Walt Disney's endearing and enduring creation and it was wonderful to see Mickey as *The Sorcerer's Apprentice*, bringing to life a musical narrative, and jokey magic, Mickey's ambitions and catastrophe for a laugh and I can still see Mickey plodding with his mop, the syncopated notes of Paul Dukas' score for Goethe's poem (I did look that up just now), dramatic and rhythmic plodding.

And you did the same, bringing out the comic and the range of dancing animals, hippopotamus (Hyacinth Hippo) ballet, ostriches, elephants and alligators for Ponchiellis' *Dance of the Hours*. Beethoven melodies have just come into the imagination, the lyrically sweet images, centaurs and Greek mythology, accompanying his *Pastoral Symphony*. And now the contrast with cosmic images, creation, evolution in the universe accompanying Stravinsky's *Rite of Spring*. Recognisable animated delight compared with abstract colours, abstract shapes for Stravinsky. But the abstract images for Bach's *Toccata and Fugue* are not there in my memory – perhaps they were too abstract for a schoolboy.

I had better bring this enjoyable self-indulgence to a close. You were brought to a close with the sinister, dark images, literally diabolical images, blackness and bright eyes, the solemn suggestions of evil with Mussorgsky's *Night on Bald Mountain*. Still sinister as I see it and hear it in my mind's eyes and ears. But redemption was fortunately at hand, the pilgrims, an atmosphere of holiness to quietly overcome the atmosphere of evil, the familiar strains of Schubert's *Ave Maria*. A final sense of peace as we left the cinema.

Yes, I have been introduced to many composers, many classics, but these came later and I've always wished that I had a greater sensibility foundation earlier in life.

But, thankfully, you were there, a powerful presence in my early years.

Dear *Winter Light*,

It is over fifty years since I first saw you, a rather bleak experience if I may say so, but more than interesting and arresting as an Ingmar Bergman film and a reminder of his Lutheran upbringing, the spiritual and theological perspectives that he brought into his life, despite his statements of loss of faith, and brought into his films. I did write a letter to *Cries and Whispers*, a wonderful vision of Lutheran religion (yes, and I did see *Fanny* and *Alexander* to try to understand him as a religious person).

One of the problems of writing to you is that your original title, *Nattvardsgasterna*, means *The Communicants*, which places the emphasis on your religious congregation, the pastor, Tomas, and the small group who attend his service. I don't know who made the decision for the title in English to be *Winter Light*, but I will go for that title in being a communicant with you.

Since you are the second part of Bergman's trilogy of the first half of the 1960s, I was tempted to write to all three films. There was the fascination of God as a spider, as well as the reference to St Paul to the Corinthians, *Through a Glass Darkly*, God's self-manifesting in madness, within such a dysfunctional family. There was less temptation to write to *The Silence*, although, I suppose, there is much to write about in a cold world where God is so completely absent.

So, a letter to you. Your setting is one day in the life of a pastor, a Sunday, a situation with which I could immediately identify – though I question the ways I could identify with you as the pastor's day goes on. Actually, one of the first things to say to you is how deceptive is that English title. While the word 'light' indicates some brightness, it is certainly modified by the word 'winter'. Winter light comes in the context of Scandinavian darkness, long nights, almost minimal light. But, of course, the title is a striking image for a pastor's faith struggle. I am not sure how much I identified with Tomas. After all, he is played by one of Bergman's most serious actors, Gunnar Bjornstrand. I just checked to see how old he was when he played this role – he was in his early 50s. That was too old for me when I first saw you in my 20s (now I have to stretch my memory to go back to my 50s!).

But as I think back, I see Tomas as a kind of priest icon. After all, the first ten minutes or so of your eighty minutes' running time, he is there presiding at Sunday ritual. He is a mediator between God and his community, communicants – even though the gathering is very small. He presides, an image of God, perhaps rather of the stern Father than of the humane Son (though he does speak later of the mystery of Christ and his suffering). It is, perhaps, difficult to see any action of the Holy Spirit.

It is not so difficult for a priest to identify with him there at the altar, sometimes wondering about the value of the rituals and ceremonies, wondering how much they affect the congregation, whether the congregation is there because of love of God or because of a sense of duty. And this has its consequences for the faith-life of a priest. As Bergman indicated, relying on the authority of St Paul, we do now see here on earth through a glass darkly. But so often, the glass is opaque. Can we really see God or is the mirror distorting God?

When I look at the faith representation of a priest/pastor in a film, I wonder about his faith in terms of something I learned in theology long since – St Augustine's categorising of faith. He noted that in faith we believe God, the truth that God reveals, a kind of dogmatic faith that seems to sustain believers in a very cerebral way. It is something of faith in a sense of duty. But, Augustine went on to say that faith is believing in God, his Latin indicating a kind of commitment to God in action. This is love of God through love of neighbour, ministry, charity... And what has just come into my memory this minute, provoked by these considerations of Augustine, is the distinction between *orthodoxy*, right-thinking, and *orthopraxis*, right-acting. (Actually, I've had a further distraction from a wise nun teaching theology where she went further and advocated *orthopoesis*, right-creating, right creativity, which ought to be fulfilment of faith.)

I hope you don't mind these theological reflections – I'm sure that Ingmar Bergman would relish this kind of conversation. And he would have relished it in the 1960s, the decade of extraordinary change, especially in Western culture, the discovery of freedoms (and indulging in them), and if not the death of God, then at least of questioning God. I have always liked the 1960s, the decade of my 20s, final commitment in my religious congregation, theological studies, ordination, ministry in school, in teaching theology...

You also remind us of the temptation to pervading pessimism in struggles with faith – a world apprehensive about the possibilities of nuclear destruction (you would have been in production and postproduction at the time of the Missiles of October, 1962). After the celebration of the ritual, Tomas is so preoccupied with his own struggles that he is ineffectual in hearing the anxieties of the fisherman, Jonas, who sees no way out but to kill himself. And the schoolteacher offering herself in love, but faith doubts and the struggle have closed Tomas to any human warmth - except that he does encounter a little boy at the schoolhouse and there is a blind faith finally on his lips.

I'd better stop now, not wanting to be too Bergmanesque. But I did see somewhere that Bergman himself said, 'I think I have made just one picture that I really like, and that is *Winter Light*. Everything is exactly as I wanted to have it, in every second of this picture'.

You have been described as a cold film. Yes, the winter light is cold but, though you do not arrive at conclusions, your light might be described as 'luminous'.

Dear *A Score to Settle*,

I should say at the outset that you are not the kind of film I usually write a Dear Letter to. But I was rather stirred as I watched you, finding a lot more value in you as your running time progressed. Then I thought I ought to look you up to see how Nicolas Cage fans responded to you – and how the Nicolas Cage non-fans, irritated by his continually acting in action-oriented films responded – I found there were mixed reactions. The comments which came from those who did not expect much from Cage or his action shows – just another one, easily dismissible. However, I was heartened to find there were others who found you, at least, above average.

I'm sure you that you would not be put out to be described as a B-budget action drama, featuring the ever-present Cage (who seems to churn out almost half a dozen of your kind of film each year for the past decade), Canada-filmed, the supporting cast of lesser or little-known names. And that title of yours, indicates a revenge film which, of course, you are.

But your writer and the director seem to have given much more attention to you than might have been expected. There is much more in the screenplay concerning characters and situations but also an ultimate challenge to our sense of realism as we watch and you shift to imaginative fantasy. You make us re-examine the truth of what we have seen. And you have quite a lot of visual flourishes that are engaging – an obvious one is the escort's scarf floating in the wind, close-up, while she and Cage take off speeding in the expensive car. But, there is much more than that.

It is true that the brutality of your opening is rather challenging. A gang boss is being coached as to how to swing a baseball pitch – and then our seeing that he is aiming at a victim, tied up, bleeding.

The central character, Frank, coaching the boss who, ultimately, bloodily bludgeons his victim with the baseball bat. And then you shift, nineteen years later, Frank in his prison cell, getting ready to leave. At this stage, you don't provide so much explanation, leaving it to us to wonder about him, especially since there is no one to meet him, who then walks along the highway, seeing someone coming towards him, finding that it is his son, Joey, and they walk along the road together, looking for their old home, Frank digging up a suitcase full of cash, and their checking into a lavish hotel. Reconciliation? A new life? Reform?

This is one of Nicolas Cage's much more restrained performances (though he does let loose with the touch of his expected maniacal outbursts later on), told by the doctor that his constant insomnia will lead to a physical collapse and his death. Has he decided to live without the revenge?

In retrospect, one of the best aspects of your screenplay is the relationship between father and son, the son who was abandoned, his mother dying, the gang bosses pledging that he will be looked after, his decline into addiction. He is initially tentative in his relationship with his father, but you show, pleasingly, the gradual growth in amicable bonding between father and son. However, just as you do this, you reveal that Frank is intent on settling his score, the fact that he resented having been abandoned in prison for so long.

As he goes to meet his former friends, we realise that, especially as he buys a gun, he still is intent on being an executioner. This is jolting for us your audience, watching the steps to revenge which we can understand but not approve of. But you are very interesting in showing Frank's continued physical collapsing, his encounter with the escort who contributes to humanising him, the disappearance of his son and his search for him, the discovery that he was deceived about the death of the boss, discovering in a scene with a compassionate nurse, that the target of his main revenge has been in coma for 15 years and did not betray his promise to look after Joey, a finale, in a church setting for a wedding, his realisation of the betrayal of his friend: and the moral of your story – what does it profit anyone to gain the whole revenge and risk the loss of their soul?

So, it looks as though I got more out of you then the action fans who were judging you merely at a basic level of action, fast pace, violence, and found you wanting.

As you might guess, I will give you a good review, but won't be giving you a recommendation that all viewers should watch you. But you do have a recommendation for those who enjoy genre films which offer some substantial themes and treatment.

Dear *Curtain: Poirot's Last Case*,

It is 9 May 2020. We have been in lockdown for eight weeks or so, Coronavirus, Covid-19.

I came across a cartoon the other day that said: 'most useless purchase 2019 – a 2020 Planner'. Who would have thought! Actually, we seem to be surviving lockdown quite well. The spread of the virus is not as extensive here as in so many other countries, especially in Europe. In fact, to this date, there are only 65 people infected in our Shire of Booroondara. The total number of dead to date it is 97 in the whole of Australia. After getting back to Australia from Europe in mid-March, I did experience 14 days of total-isolation (getting somewhat used to it by the second week), so that lockdown doesn't seem so restricting. I enjoyed a tram ride to a doctor's appointment last week, the first in two months. We can go for a walk in a nearby park – although the avoidance of greetings from passers-by seems to indicate that many think the virus is communicated by eye-to-eye contact.

Which means then that most of us have more time to look at the television screen (while regretting the cinema closure and anticipating the huge pileup of films, new and big films, when social distancing is not so obligatory – whenever that will be). The Foxtel Sleuth Channel is playing an Agatha Christie's Poirot mystery every day and I'm nearly halfway through. There are seventy titles, many short stories, many full-length features. But, that you know. And, there is David Suchet. What got me started was a weekend festival in April with David Suchet introducing ten films, including you.

The thought had gone through my mind that I should write to at least one of the David Suchet Poirot mysteries – and because you are the final one, also the last in Agatha Christie's Poirot novels, it seemed best to write to you. When you were released in 2013, David Suchet was 67 (and, when he introduced the series on television, he was 73). Which meant that when he made his first Poirot television film in 1989, he was 43. That means he was Poirot for a quarter of a century.

The thing is that you are not quite typical of the series. And there was the temptation to watch you when you were screened, earlier than many others, short stories and full-length films. The curiosity turned out to be overwhelming. What was Poirot's last case? How did he handle it? How did he die?

I enjoyed the device of Poirot being at Styles, the venue of the first case with Captain Hastings. And after so many decades, some angles on that mysterious case, there were still some repercussions to be discovered. And there was great pleasure in seeing Hugh Fraser again, also 25 years older now (and a year older than David Suchet in fact).

For two thirds of your running time, I was becoming a bit disappointed. Yes, Poirot was older, unwell, speculating about death. The murder came late and, while Poirot did some questioning, he was not always to the fore. And then he died. But I realised there was still one third of your running time to go. And, in a way, that was a stroke of genius. Poirot had left a manuscript for Hastings to read, explaining all that had happened. And finally, after he was shown dead, he did come to the fore on screen again, and ingenious explanations, a twist, and behaviour that ran the risk of being morally reprehensible. Perhaps it was. Poirot's Catholicism emerging more strongly at the end, praying his rosary, talking about God's will and forgiveness.

Then I noticed that some of the viewers were not happy with you at all, especially Poirot's deception, his using Captain Hastings, the revelation that he was not quite as infirm as he suggested, that he not only unmasked the killer but taunted him, threatened him, and executed him. There were many cries of moral outrage and indignation. Some even suggested that Agatha Christie was being cynical in her ending the life and career of her detective. If life is to be seen in black and white, that could be a conclusion.

However, life is in colour as you are (although the brightness is frequently muted throughout, night sequences, dark corridors...). Which means then that Poirot, still seeking justice, realises that the murderer could go scot-free and that it was his duty to kill him. The actual scene and the direct shot to the temple is quite cold-blooded.

I have, we all have, enjoyed the eccentricities of Poirot, Belgian, ('I am not a little French frog, I am a little Belgian frog'), fastidious and fussy, relying on Hastings so often as his unimaginative assistant (whom Agatha Christie herself described as 'something of a dunderhead'), teasing Miss Lemon and working for years with the often uncomprehending Chief Inspector Japp, tributes to Hugh Fraser and Philip Jackson and Pauline Moran, intricate cases, malicious motivations, extraordinary deceptions, often exotic locations, the twists and turns of malevolence, his grey cells pondering the clues, his unmasking the villains - and so many rather conceited self-congratulations but with such charm that he too can be forgiven. At one stage, however, Agatha Christie did write in her journal that she found Poirot 'bombastic, detestable, tiresome!'

Glad to tell you that there are still quite a number of episodes to catch up on but, with lockdown, I may have seen them all by the end of June.

P.S. There was a second wave of the virus in Melbourne, another six weeks of lockdown, obligatory wearing of masks – and finishing the Poirot series by the end of July! Then lockdown was extended, even more strictly, until the end of October, one of the longest lockdowns in the world up till then.

Dear *Okoributo*, Dear *Departures*,

Let me tell you at once that you are a fine, often beautiful, film to be recommended.

However, your audiences might be wondering during your first ten minutes. You begin slowly and solemnly with ceremonial and ritual for the dead. Then, without warning, you become quite farcical and we wonder where we are. This is pre-credits. And immediately after the credits, there is an orchestra playing Beethoven's *Ode to Joy* with a full choir. Who are you? What are the departures?

Actually, your central character, the young Daigo, a cello player whose orchestra is shut down, wonders about this same question. When he applies for a job on returning to his home town, he thinks he will work for a travel agent or be a tour guide. The Japanese title of the film is said to mean, 'the one who sees persons off...'. But, in fact, he is to be a 'coffinator', an embalmer of the dead who performs his duties with religious atmosphere, reverent ceremonial and a decorum that enables the grieving family and mourners to pay their respects to the dead and experience the solemnity of the final rite of passage. Death is seen, in Buddhist and eastern religion terms, not as the end but as the gateway to the next stage of existence. Death is a gateway and we will all meet again.

I became fascinated with the repetition of this ceremony, the ritual meticulously the same, respect for the dead, the religious beliefs, the attention to detail, the washing of the body, clothing the body, the garment, the makeup, the special clothes or things associated with the deceased, the reverent placing of the hands, the interment in the coffin, burial and cremation. But the response of the mourners so different – and we realise that the manager and Daigo are contributing to a sense of human dignity and an acknowledgment of the life of the dead person as well as the survivors.

That all sounds very, very serious, and so it is. However, your screenplay is interspersed with a great deal of humour, especially in Daigo's personal journey from being very sick at his first case to a final ritual which brings the whole drama, the embalming, his marriage, his family and the absence of his father, to a very satisfying conclusion.

I was not familiar with the actors but I found that Masahiro Matoko gave a finely nuanced performance, just the right seriousness and comedy, an acute sense of timing and facial expressions indicating the depths of his character. Tustomu Yamizaki brought a blend of the offhand and the dedicated to his role as the manager.

And you are beautiful to look at (which is sometimes rather challenging through our tears). You are a wonderful combination of the realistically mundane, the sadness of life and its uncertainties, yet the funny side of human foibles, the emotion of music and an opportunity (without being preached at) for the audience to really respond emotionally to and intellectually think about the deeper aspects of life and death.

In fact, there is so much to remember – Daigo and tensions with his father, love for his mother, his relationship with his wife, the presence of the cello and his playing.

Looking back at this description, I do sound as if I am being carried away (and, I suppose, in the cinema I was).

I had better tell you about the situation where I saw you. It was in Washington DC. Our Catholic Jury Prize for SIGNIS was being awarded for the first time, 2009. You were the opening film. Our jury was rather overwhelmed and, though we saw quite a number of fine films in the next days, the sense of being overwhelmed remained with us. I had the pleasure of announcing that you were our winner. Perhaps we were something of a prelude because you then won the Oscar for Best Foreign Language Film. I am glad to be able to tell you that you appear at times on our World Movies television channel.

So you are a film of Japanese culture, yet a film of human nature, human sensitivity with a universal appeal.

Dear *Duel*,

It was in 1973 that I saw you at the Croydon drive-in, possibly as a supporting feature. How could I know that you would become something of classic or that your director, Steven Spielberg, would go on to achieve so much in the next almost half-century? But you certainly made an impression. I just glanced at the opening of my review back then, '*Duel* is an unexpectedly excellent film, a parable about modern man, relevant and unpretentious'. I see that I wrote 'man' – those were the days before inclusive language! But, all things considered, not a bad opening line for a review of a brief film, made for television, playing at the drive-in.

While Steven Spielberg has been the star film director, a great deal of credit goes to his screenwriter, the celebrated Richard Matheson, with a penchant for science fiction enabling him to explore allegories of what it is to be human, of human nature.

I see that I use the word 'parable'. In a way, that was immediately evident by the decision to call the hero, 'David Mann'. Most audiences immediately saw the connection with David and Goliath (the oil tanker, belching smoke, was an anonymous giant figure to be fought, to use wits against, to be conquered. The classic usage means that we have to use the title 'Everyman' (Everyperson sounding rather ungainly.) But David Mann is a typical American Everyman for male audiences to identify with, an invitation for everyone, male or female, to identify with him, at least in this situation, harassed in his car.

I just checked to see what age Dennis Weaver was when he played David Mann. He was 37 when you were released. Just right. He played a middle-aged businessman, going to an appointment, but like any day, a clash with his wife, harassed, feeling the pressure. He wasn't ready for a duel on the highway. And, when it happened unexpectedly, he was taken aback, faced to take stock of himself and how he should react in this threatening situation.

I finished the first draft of this letter and then went back to my 1973 review – I think I got it right, 'until he is a victim of his own irrational but credible fear and the lure of outwitting the danger and his opponent'. To that extent, I suppose, you offer a cinematic examination of conscience for all adults in the audience. Most people can identify with a driver, with difficulties on the road, experience some road rage, forcible or mild, having to keep an eye on the road, to deal with difficult driving on the part of the attacker as well as for oneself. (Actually, for me and the others in the audience at the drive-in, we were sitting, observing, identifying, in our cars, we had driven to the cinema, the wheel in front of us was tangible, our feet near the clutch and the brakes.)

And soon the challenge to conscience was: how would I react to this menacing driver? Would I let him be? Ignore him? Let him race on? Would I allow myself to be provoked? Irritated? Angry? Competitive? Vengeful? And we share this with David Mann, going through all these emotions and challenges.

My memories after all these decades, before I watched you again on Movie Greats, was of the road, the car, the overbearing truck, swerving, stopping and waiting, menacing, aggressively turning back, the anonymity of the driver, the pursuit. The scenes with David Mann back with other people had faded from memory, but rather jolted back as I watched you again. I hadn't realised that your portrait of other people showed them to be either aggressive, fearful, offhand or apathetic, no great help in a crisis. Off the road, your most tense moments were in the diner, David Mann being introspective, acquired interior voice-over (or better, voice-under) revealing the fear, the uncertainty, the glancing at all the potential drivers, his brash and rash confrontation, the physical fight, his being mistaken as he was ousted from the diner. I felt sympathy for the bus driver trying to get his vehicle back on the road, dealing with the rather obnoxious children, chattering, poking faces at David Mann, certainly not charming, childlike innocents.

So, what were you saying about human nature? Something of a grim commentary.

As your tension mounts, and the musical score emphasises the beats, the rhythms, speed, the final examination of conscience question arises. How will David trick and destroy Goliath? In fact, Goliath destroys himself, becoming smug? Too self-confident? Underestimating his opponent? Classic hubris? And great was the fall, literally, thereof!

So what do Matheson and Spielberg leave us with? In our consciences? In our identification with David Mann? Triumphant? Relief? Mixed laughter? Any regrets? Or just sitting as the sun sets, on the cliff, contemplating what has happened, no immediate answer...?

And you ask all of this in just ninety minutes.

Dear *Glory*,

Excitement, as I remember, is one of the main feelings I had as I watched you, being taken into a particular time, a particular place, places, the Civil War. In fact, it is now just over 30 years since I saw you, November 1989. And I saw you in the United States, in New York City, coming to the end of a wonderful sabbatical year there.

And I was ready to see you because of a lot of the reading that I did during that sabbatical, most of all, John Jakes' *North and South*, as well as the many historical novels from the American Revolution to the 20th century by Gore Vidal. And what was important for me was not that I read them sitting in my room at the rectory of St Elizabeth in Washington Heights, New York, but, rather, reading them during Greyhound bus tours (just $135 for seven days travel in those days!). The main trip, capitalising on the full seven days, took me through New Jersey into Pennsylvania, into Ohio and Kentucky, then south into Tennessee, Arkansas and Mississippi, coming back north to Missouri, zigzagging between Nebraska and Iowa, North and South Dakota. Then, perhaps a little anti-climax, through Minnesota, Wisconsin into Illinois. But travelling by bus took us into the cities and towns, main streets and side streets, neighbourhoods where no train could venture.

Later, a trip took me self into Virginia, North and South Carolina and as far as Savannah, Georgia. Visiting Charleston, South Carolina, certainly brought the Civil War into greater consciousness, travelling on the harbour, seeing Fort Sumpter.

But part of the exhilaration in seeing you was that we were invited to see the action of the Civil War from two perspectives. When we identified with Colonel Robert Shaw, embodied by Matthew Broderick, wounded in battle, recuperating, then taking charge of the 54th region Regiment of black soldiers, we see events and characters through white eyes. But the intense focus on the soldiers, embodied by Denzel Washington, Morgan Freeman, Andre Braugher, their experiences of service, hardships and injury, war and death, the descendants of slaves fighting for the Union, invited us to see events and characters through African-American eyes.

Important for me was seeing the abolitionist, Frederick Douglass, a dignified Raymond St Jacques, his place in Northern society, his campaigns, drawing on the slave history, visions of freedom and equality.

For an outsider to the United States, having the unexpected value of living there for a year, your credentials were important. Screenplay is well researched, drawing on *One Gallant Rush* by Peter Burchard (1965) and *Lay this Laurel* by Lincoln Kirstein (1974) as well the letters of its principal protagonist, Colonel Shaw. The Civil War has been the setting for a great number of movies from *Gone with the Wind* to *The Good, The Bad and the Ugly* to *Cold Mountain*. There have been screen versions of classics as well which depict the war, like *The Red Badge of Courage*, or have the civil war as background, like *Little Women*. Ken Burns directed the Emmy and Humanitas prize-winning, ten-hour mini series for television entitled *The Civil War* in 1990. Ronald F. Maxwell made the five-hour long *Gettysburg* in 1993, told from the Union perspective, and followed it with *Gods and Generals* in 2003, about the major battles leading up to Gettysburg from the perspective of the South.

What remains in my memory and imagination after three decades is, of course, the impact of the battles, the troops, attack, gunshot and explosions, injury and deaths. And Shaw himself is killed. But, from the 1980s and into the present, there is a significant memory of the troops, marching, sometimes downtrodden, even the lash, but discovering that they had a greater place in United American society. Denzel Washington (winning his first Oscar as Best Supporting Actor) and Morgan Freeman were in the process of becoming screen icons.

I say this with some ruefulness. It is June 2020. There have been over two weeks of powerful riots all over the United States, extending to countries beyond, protest gatherings in Australia, despite the covid-19 pandemic. There is a huge crying out, outcry, 'Black Lives Matter'. *Glory*, your story and themes continue to have a resonance today, as we wonder what racial equality in the United States (and in Australia) will turn out to be.

Dear *Erin Brockovich*,

So this is what an American environmental champion looks like. Actually, I should have said 'warrior'. Once she had lost her accident damages claim in court, she was on the move, on the attack, skirmishes then battles to win – for ordinary people. And righteously beyond warrior, crusader!

You would admit that Erin was one of those people who deserves – 'don't judge a book by its cover'. What is immediately striking about her is her choice of outfits. Somebody remarked of her blouses, skirts, trousers, sweaters that they are 'trailer-trash' outfits. She is criticised at the legal office for her style and told to lose the clothes. She responds that she wears things because she thinks she looks nice.

And, of course, your star is Julia Roberts. Looks and outfits. (And then multi-awards and an Oscar.)

I think what gripped many audiences – and me – twenty years ago was that Erin seemed so unlikely in the role. She herself would have originally thought that. Untrained, but with hidden reserves of intelligence (which everyone underestimates because of her provocative and sexy wardrobe, twice-divorced with three children). But you show that heroic action begins with asking questions even if you don't have any idea of the answers or where they might lead. So yours is a social justice story, she initially asking about an anomaly in the firm's files. Then a meeting with over six hundred people affected by chromium poisoning from Pacific Gas and Electricity in the water, a class action for more than 300 million dollars and a new life for Erin, and busy. Busy.

Yours is also a David and Goliath story. Erin also discovered that she was worth something in herself and that with energy and compassion (and some aggression, actually worth quite a lot) she could help people, showing up the professionals whose skills were not exactly people-oriented. In that sense, your story is inspiring. With the welter of photos of the real Erin at the time of your release in 2000, one is able to say that she is a flamboyant personality. One commentator remarked that, having met the real Erin, he realised that Julia Roberts had underplayed her!

Erin Brockovich comes across as extremely outgoing. She does not seem to have developed an inner life. She is energised by her relationships, by her children, by the effort of keeping going every day with little money to support her. She tries to be inventive during the job application interviews with which the movie begins. And she can't keep quiet in the court room when she defends herself against slurs in her case for the accident insurance claim. And this is her style right the way through, sometimes getting into trouble for being too 'out there', but also using this energy in her dealings with the people in the class action.

It is no secret that her decisions are subjective. She personalises everything. Her love for her children and her care for their welfare are the main criteria by which she acts. She brings this same engagement to her contacts with her clients. We can't but admire her.

Given her interest in the file she was given to put away, her inner life awakens: curiosity, sense of justice, a sense of crusading. Her son complains that she reads documents during the meals. And she starts to move into action, decisive action to help all those people duped by the energy company. Once on the case, her energy seems boundless (which still seems to be true of the actual Erin Brockovich).

This seriousness and concern seems to take over in her work. She pursues the documents, realising the consequences for the court. She is a woman of her word in guaranteeing the rights of her clients. And with Ed Masery, she becomes a skilled legal advocate. Not that she loses her personalised approach to decisions.

It seems to me that you serve as a parable because you take your audience into what seems a familiar world of ordinary people, some down on their luck, others with professional careers and others who have become victims of environmental fraud. Erin Brockovich 'subverts' this world, revealing the unlikely Erin as a saviour figure, someone who embodies (though she might be surprised to hear it) the qualities of the Gospel.

I am particularly remembering the sequence where Erin and Ed meet the top lawyers in their office, a formal place with formal dress codes and expectations of legal professionalism and the assistant patronises Erin about the details of her files and Erin confounds her by knowing the phone numbers off by heart as well knowing the names of all her clients and the details of their life stories. A reminder that leadership is not all objective efficiency but personal affirmation of clients as well.

I like Erin Brokovich. And I like the way you tell her story. She is an unexpected heroine (American out-there style). If she was needed in the 1990s, she is certainly needed in these more desperate environment-challenged times.

Dear *Dead Man Walking*,

You were a surprise to me when you were released in 1995. It was the year of the centenary of cinema and I had been asked to write about the changing image of priests on screen. In the article, I noted that with the changes in style and community life of congregations of sisters, as well as fewer numbers joining, there would be fewer films about nuns. I was not entirely wrong, but you provided an immediate challenge. You are a fine film, understanding religious vocation and ministry, paying tribute to the work and life of American sisters – and worldwide.

During 1995, you made so many Catholics and non-Catholics around the world aware of Sister Helen Prejean, the American Sister of St Joseph working in Louisiana. She would never have dreamed when she made her vows as a nun (which we can see in the flashback footage of ceremonies used during your opening) that she would have become something of a household name forty years later. And as I'm writing to you, a further twenty-five years later. Her prison ministry, through her campaigning, her articles and books, the documentaries, the feature film and the opera, became widely-known in the mid-1990s and has given encouragement and hope to those facing the issues of capital punishment. I remember being very pleased, watching the Oscar ceremony in April 1996, that she sat in the front row of the theatre beside Susan Sarandon, seen worldwide by millions as the actress paid tribute to the nun in her Oscar acceptance speech.

For anyone wondering about changes in religious life for women after the Second Vatican Council, you provide a very helpful narrative overview.

In adapting Helen Prejean's book, Tim Robbins – in a labour of love of writing and direction – combined stories of two prisoners on death row into the character of Matthew Poncelet (a completely convincing Sean Penn). Poncelet writes to Sister Helen who is teaching underprivileged children and asks her to be his spiritual director in the weeks before his execution. When she goes to visit him, not knowing what to expect, she is caught up in the Gospel teachings of forgiveness of sinners (seven times seventy) and the image of Jesus on the cross pardoning the repentant thief and promising him paradise that day. The priest chaplain is not impressed, preferring to tick her off on the issue of whether she is wearing a traditional nun's habit or not. Her community, however, are supportive, even being prepared to make available one of the order's plots for Poncelet to be buried in. The sisters also join in protests against capital punishment as does the local bishop. Her ministry leads her in two directions: quality of life, forgiveness and reconciliation.

You show how she is first drawn to the spiritual accompaniment of the prisoners. Whatever they have done, they have the right to pardon by God and to trying to repair in some ways the brutality they have perpetrated. This is a ministry of discernment. Sister Helen has to listen attentively to the words and to the heart of Matthew Poncelet. If she is to succeed in bringing any quality into the final part of his life, she has to be a catalyst for grace. He has to acknowledge truly and profoundly what he has done, the cruelty towards his victims which, in his case, are both the violation of rape and the ultimate violation of life in murder. She has to foster his sense of repentance, of sorrow, of the need for some kind of confession, of absolution from God, from her, from his victims and from their families, for some kind of atonement and reconciliation.

Dramatically speaking, Tim Robbins has made a judicious decision to include the flashbacks to the actual crime at this point of the film. They become part of Poncelet's confession. As we see what he did, we know that he is truly remembering and acknowledging the profound and care-less evil of what he has done. It is visually shocking. Confession is not merely a matter of words (which are always easier to hear than the visual impact of seeing crimes like these in action). For Poncelet, this confession to Sister Helen is a conversion in the best sense. Profound sin can be described as an 'aversion' from right and good and from God. It is a complete aversion, a turning away. Profound repentance can be described, therefore, as a 'conversion' to right and good and to God. It is a complete conversion, a turning towards...

Ultimately, Matthew Poncelet does confess to her and if ever there was a cinema moment when the giving of sacramental absolution by any minister, irrespective of whether that person be a priest or not cried out for blessing, this is it. Yet, as a nun, all she can offer is prayerful forgiveness. Even state rules forbid her to include any hymns in these final prayers before execution because the music could stir emotional response that would be detrimental to the execution processes. When Sister Helen sings one of the hymns by the St Louis Jesuits, *Be Not Afraid*, well known to so many Catholics, it is a scene of love and reconciliation, of courage in faith before death. She tells him to look at her because she will be for him the face of love as he dies.

You use a dramatic device to open your audiences' eyes to look further than Matthew Poncelet. Sister Helen's eyes are opened in an unexpectedly emotional way. While we are shown the grief of the Poncelet family, especially Matthew's mother and what the shame of the crime and the pain of the execution mean to her, the screenplay at first gives minimum attention to the families of the victims. It is only when Sister Helen goes to see them out of courtesy that she is made to realise that she has neglected her ministry to the survivors of Poncelet's crimes. They assume that, especially as a nun, she has come to comfort them, to be on their side. The Percys are angry with her, accuse her of arrogance and order her to leave their house. So far, your audience has been caught up in her prison ministry and the good she could do for the prisoners. We have overlooked the families, just as she has. The scenes of her dealing with the families, their disillusionment when they judge that she is ministering to 'the enemy' are harrowing for her and for those in the audience who realise that crime affects more than the immediate victims and the perpetrators. Her horizons, and ours, have to widen. Even more demands are made on compassion.

This plot thread comes to its climax when members of the victims' families attend the execution. They have not been able to share the same perspective as Sister Helen. Perhaps their feelings for vengeance have been tempered to feelings for justice. Poncelet attempts to convey something of his repentance and need for their forgiveness but they have not reached that point. Before he is strapped, Poncelet extends his arms in the form of a cross. We are reminded of Calvary, that Jesus gave his life on the cross for all – including the repentant thief.

What is significant and is something that gives you an even greater spiritual depth as well as challenge to the audience is your final sequence. The camera tracks outside a church. As we look in, we see Sister Helen and Mr Delacroix, the father of the boy (who has listened to Sister Helen but has not been able to bring himself to forgive, who has attended the execution) both kneeling in prayer. If the final virtue in the seamless garment of life is reconciliation between those who have been enemies which leads towards peace, then you provide a perfect ending.

Dear *Les Innocentes*,

You made a powerful impact on me at first sight. It was in 2016. For me, it was very significant that 2016 saw two films which explored Catholic themes in a profound way. There was Martin Scorsese's *Silence*, the story of the Jesuits in Japan in the 17th century and the fidelity of the laity, even to martyrdom, as well as issues of challenges to faith. Then there was you – the harrowing story of a convent of Polish sisters who were abused and raped by invading Russian soldiers during World War II and have to deal with the aftermath in terms of location and faith.

You are a French/Polish production, a French director, Anne Fontaine, and two French actors but production and the rest of the cast Polish, a stark picture of Poland and the Polish countryside in the post-war winter of 1945.

You and *Silence* are powerful reminders of Catholic sensibilities, Catholic sensitivities and the depth of Catholic themes. One theme is that of convent life in the 20th century. Audiences who remember the 1959 *The Nuns' Story*, will note the similarities in the life of the nuns in the convent of the 1940s, contemplative, enclosed, austere, penitential, an emphasis on obedience, of the vows, the dominating role of the superior. I realise that this kind of religious life is only memory for older audiences, very much a surprise for younger audiences – although there are pockets of religious communities like this around the world today. The stone convent looks grim, the main action takes place in winter, the audience is taken into the chapel frequently for the chanting of the Office, to the corridors, the cells, the refectory. I find it amazing to remember that in exactly twenty years, the sessions of the Second Vatican Council would be completed and profound (and unimagined) changes in convent life were in the offing.

The impact of the rape story is disturbing, the horror for innocent women, nuns, virgins, with the physical experience of the assault, with the psychological impact of the violation. You show the nuns reticent about their condition, embarrassed, some mystified by their experience, a sense of shame, a sense of self-blame, the concealing of pregnancy beneath ample habits, moral issues with which the sisters have to cope.

I am just thinking now of what your impact must be on a women's audience, speaking so directly to their sensibilities and sensitivities. I realise how important you are to a men's audience, shocking us, challenging us to empathy and understanding.

In wartime, in the convent propriety, I was intrigued by the perspective of the superior, wanting to keep the reputation of the convent respectable, concealing what had happened, stating that she was adopting out the babies, something which is not true. Rather, she baptises the babies and leaves them by the wayside crosses. And while she does mellow in some ways, it is discovered that she has been infected by the Russians with syphilis.

But you are a film not without hope. One of the sisters leaves the convent to find some medical help, from the French doctors and nurses present in the Polish village to tend to French wounded before they are repatriated. Your focus then is on a French nurse (and the film based on her memoir of these events before she died, prematurely, in 1946). Intriguingly, she has a Communist background and so the convent tends to be alien territory. As portrayed by Lou de Laage, she is a fine woman, a volunteer, a woman of concern and compassion, engaging with the liaison Sister Maria (Agata Buzek) who speaks French and becomes more and more frank in her discussions with the nurse.

You show Sister Maria learning a great deal of medical skills as well as compassion from the nurse and begins to confide in her, even more sympathetic with the sisters when she herself is attacked and threatened by a Russian convoy, sharing the rape-impact on the nuns, then enlisting the help of a Red Cross doctor who is Jewish, his family killed in Auschwitz and who interprets the reaction of the superior as anti-Semitic, but he assists with the births.

As the time came to give birth, many of the sisters are fearful, ashamed, prudish and ignorant. Each of the sisters reacts in her own way, some avoiding the reality, others conscious of their becoming mothers. (You realise that in later decades, issues of the appropriateness of abortion in such circumstances were raised in moral and theological discussions. In the last twenty years, there have also been quite a number of films about women who were raped in the Balkan wars of the 1990s, questions of abortion, issues of raising the children and the consequences for the children and their origins and legitimacy in Balkan society.)

It is the nurse herself who comes up with a solution which is positive for the sisters as mothers and for the local orphans who have been seen playing in and wandering the streets.

In fact, you are a film of faith but, ultimately, of hope and charity, finally symbolised by a charming group photo of the sisters, the children, and the visitors who have been able to come, at last, for the profession of vows by the novices.

My experience of seeing you (the title innocents being the sisters as well as the babies) was, at times, emotionally harrowing, always morally challenging, probing the meaning of innocence, suffering and the place and role of God, of faith. Thank you.

Dear *It Must be Heaven*,

Do you show Heaven? Not quite. But you do raise the question: can there be peace on earth? And can there be peace on earth for the Palestinians?

Through you, this is a letter to your writer-director-performer, Elia Suleiman (Dear Elia, if you get to read this letter). I have enjoyed his droll political comedy, partly deadpan (especially his facial expressions – I mean lack of facial expressions), partly satire and parody, partly gentle about human nature. But, all the time, he is also making political points. He reminds us that everywhere in the world has its Palestinian situations, dread and power, acknowledgment and disregard. I enjoyed the other two films of his that I have seen, discovering him in 2002 when I responded so well to *Divine Intervention*, then, in 2009, *The Time that Remains*.

Am I right in remembering that the only word you have Elia saying (answering a friendly black cab driver in New York City is 'Nazareth'. Which is where Elia comes from, a Palestinian from his home town of Nazareth which he does enjoy featuring in your early section. (Actually, the driver asked whether Nazareth was a country.)

When I first saw *Divine Intervention*, I had had the opportunity (more pilgrimage than tourism) to visit Israel, January 1979. I suppose I had been aware of the situation in that rather small strip of land between the Mediterranean and the Jordan. I received something of a jolt when seven of us travelled in a cheroot from Jerusalem to Galilee and the Israeli military checkpoints stopped us seven times during the trip – and I was blamed by my fellow-pilgrims because my hair (1970s longer) and beard were darker, making me look like an obvious terrorist suspect. Seeing you in 2020 reminded me that I had been in Israel and in the occupied territories in 2012, three decades and more later, for a Peace Conference at the University of Jerusalem. And I had gazed at the Wall, gone through the turnstiles to the other side, the Wall, higher than I imagined, longer and more separating than I would wish, along the road to Bethlehem and finding passport control rougher and more dismissive in coming back in to Israel.

Which meant I watched you with greater interest and, I hope, empathy.

You set a tone at the beginning with a religious ceremony, robed Greek Orthodox clergy, the faithful, many of them very young, a cross and a symbolic knocking at the door of the tomb – but the man behind the door is refusing to open, the celebrant taking off his crown, going behind the scenes, sounds of a fistfight, the door opening and the celebrant summoning the faithful in. I was not (never) sure what it means but it does set your comic tone.

Then you go to Elia's own Nazareth. He is ES, alone in his apartment, wandering the streets, sitting in cafes, observing and contemplating. visiting his wife's grave, exploring the countryside. And sudden interludes when some violent young men seem to threaten him in the street, but then run past him. Intimations of terror in the streets.

Then he flies to Paris – nervously looking out the window at what seems to be a shuddering wing. However, he becomes a tourist in Paris, (which is frequently shown as deserted), the audience wandering and observing with him, the monuments, the sites, a menacing stranger staring at him in the metro, police on skates, glimpses of a file of tanks, beggars in the street served food by workers driving an ambulance, nuns serving at an outdoor soup kitchen, a priest standing smoking and observing, all kinds of detail. However, we discover his purpose in visiting Paris is to raise money for a film about Palestine, with a lot of discussion about how such a film could be made, how polemic it should be, how political – or rather should it be simply showing a character like ES visiting France and the US observing the world and intimating comparisons with Nazareth. Says the producer, 'Not Palestinian enough'.

Because the US is his next destination, similar kinds of tourism and observing, an encounter with Gael Garcia Bernal as he goes to discuss production finance in New York City – and failing again. This time, you have more explicit references to Palestine, a strong rally of exiled Palestinians, a conference and his sitting on a panel.

I did think of Jacques Tati as I began to watch ES and then discovered that practically every reviewer and blogger makes the comparison with the French comedies of Tati, especially his character, Monsieur Hulot. Tati, early in his career, tall and gaunt, Elia rather shorter, a touch more rotund, distinctive with rather shabbier clothes, always a coat, always a hat. He is in middle-age. He is bearded, bespectacled, silent. Tati was a master of mime in the eccentricities of ordinary situations. So too, Elia's ES, with his hands always behind his back, like Tati. But he generally stands, sits, observes. He can be described as enigmatic, quizzical, a spectator curious about the human race. (Commentators invoke Buster Keaton and deadpan – but that didn't occur to me!)

So I very much enjoyed your comedy – and was frequently provoked about the plight of Palestinians. One commentator remarked that you are comedy of the absurd. You are. However, there was an addition: 'absolute nonsense' – but in the best sense.

Dear *Incendies*,

On your release in 2010, you seemed to be an important film taking your audience into the upheavals and civil wars in the Middle East and some of the human and inhuman consequences that can baffle, even frighten, those of us who live comfortable lives. While the country is not named in the film, it is based on events in Lebanon, civil wars, religious wars.

You obviously made a wide impression including nomination as the Canadian entry for the 2010 Academy Awards for Best Foreign Language Film.

It really surprised me to find that you were based on a play and, in fact, there are many powerful dialogue sequences. However, the play is opened up cinematically (and vividly), with a great deal of location photography (Jordan standing in for Lebanon) and local cultural atmosphere.

Initially, you are quite a challenge. But you do offer chapter headings which help us get and maintain our bearings. Initial mystery with the boy, the tattoo on his foot, being shaved, prepared for military action, at such a young age. We have to keep our wits about us as your drama moves between two different time zones. A mother's will being read to her twin children by the lawyer for whom she has been secretary for eighteen years since she arrived with her children in Montreal. She has letters for them asking them to deliver them to their father and to their brother whom they do not know. Intriguing, especially about the brother – shocking at the final discovery and recognition.

In the present, you show the search, first of all by the daughter, Jeanne, and then by Simon, the brother, helped by their lawyer.

Modern Canadians, unused to the Middle East, go on a journey of discovery and new cultural awareness.

In the meantime, we see the past, from the 1960s to the 1990s, the life of the mother which turns out to be surprising to the children as they piece together what happened to her – and to us, because it is a frightening story. You are a story of family shame and denunciation, a woman, her lover, the birth of the boy with the tattoo on his foot, family vindictiveness and killing in the mountains of Lebanon, honour, religious and cultural clash. You are a story of adoption and the hard and unexpected life of an orphan at the time of civil war and atrocities. You are a story of a woman who receives an education but who takes a stand in the civil unrest and acts on it leading to an atrocious prison experience, years of confinement, torture, rape.

You immerse us in the past story, step by step, as the younger generation pursue it, Jeanne with intensity, Simon unwillingly. Where it leads we did not anticipate at all though as it unfolds, we might suspect what happened – and hope that it didn't. But it did.

A worst possible solution to the search and the twins having to live with it and the consequences.

You also alerted us to the talent of your director, Denis Villeneuve (whose subsequent career has not disappointed us). Your issues are important and raise our consciousness of events still being played out in the Middle East in a harrowing way.

Even writing this letter to you, expressing appreciation for what you have shown us, is a chilling experience.

Dear *Irving Berlin: An American Song*,

This is the first letter I have written to a documentary film – and, I suppose, I am writing to Irving Berlin indirectly through you.

I don't know which Irving Berlin song made a first impact on me. I can remember going to see *Annie Get Your Gun* at the St James Theatre in Elizabeth Street in Sydney, 1950. (And one of the reasons for remembering is that it was the first time that Philip and I were allowed to travel on the tram by ourselves, usually our grandmother taking us to the pictures.) Somehow or other, *White Christmas*, *Easter Parade*, seem to have always been in the memory.

I remember being very impressed with someone noting how Irving Berlin's lyrics were straightforward, like ordinary spoken conversation. (This was in contrast to the cleverly ingenious, verbal and rhythm-smart, lyrics of the songs of Cole Porter.) I was later to learn that George Gershwin praised Irving Berlin for his creativity with the American vernacular, reaching the heart and soul of America. Just thinking of some of the titles from *Annie Get Your Gun* is a fine reminder, 'Anything you can do, I can do better...' or 'The girl that I marry will have to be'..., or the anthem, 'There's No Business like Show Business' (and as I write, it's Ethel Merman belting it out with raucous tunefulness).

But you were able to incorporate all these songs into your biography of Irving Berlin. As you presented his early life story, born in the Russian empire (in what is now Belarus), the family migrating to the US, living in lower New York, eking out a living, it is the archetypal story of the Jewish refugee from Russian pogroms to Ellis Island and a new life in the United States. So, Irving Berlin, the archetypal story of rags to riches. (And I like his story because of its straightforwardness, his talent and life, so different from the struggling, sometimes bitterly dominating success of the Hollywood moguls like the Warners, Louis B. Mayer, Samuel Goldwyn.)

Watching you, I remembered that I never had any real education in music, popular or classic. I did learn to play the piano up to 4th grade, passing, then stopping at the age of 12. So while I can be led into some appreciation of classical music, I'm rather stuck in my time, my earlier times, popular songs with tunes, with melodies, especially from the US in the first half of the 20th century – the Gershwins, Jerome Kern (and Kern's encomium that Irving Berlin has no place in American music – he is American music.)

Just to confirm this, after I had watched you by chance on You Tube, I got into bed and was about to turn the lights out when Andrew Ford's *Music Show* on the ABC came on the air at 11:05 PM. It was a complete program about Irving Berlin, an interview with his biographer, James Kaplan, a good summary of what I had so liked when watching and listening to you.

There was the explanation of *Alexander's Ragtime Band* so early in Berlin's life. There were the Broadway shows of the 1920s, the lull in creativity when he went to Hollywood, yet the musicals of the mid-to-late 30s and Fred Astaire. I really enjoyed Berlin singing (definitely not his forte) making a rat-a-tat rhythm with 'How I hate to get up in the morning', his experience of World War I military life. But he also created *God Bless America* which was a theme for World War II – and his service at that time with *This is The Army*, touring to entertain the troops for several years.

I was going to mention earlier but will do so now, the pathos that you brought to the storytelling of Berlin's life, his happy marriage to the 20-year-old Dorothy Goetz and the pathos of her contracting typhoid fever during the honeymoon in Havana and her death within six months. So very sad. And then the story of his marriage to Ellen, his eloping with her after the disapproval by her father, her father disinheriting her, and Berlin giving the royalties to *Always* as a wedding gift to her. And then, more emotional devastation, the cot death of their firstborn son, Irving Berlin Jr, after only one month of life.

After the war, *Annie Get Your Gun*, Berlin asked to write because of the death of intended composer, Jerome Kern. Then the cheerfulness of *Call Me Madam*. Ethel Merman yelling again. But Berlin was a composer of the first half of the 20th century and not really in tune with the changes from the 1950s, thinking of rock 'n' roll and of Elvis Presley.

Actually, you provided a bit of a shock when you remind us that Irving Berlin died as late as 1989, aged 101.

Many thanks. You provided me with 100 minutes of entertainment, joy, nostalgia. And I did lie in bed listening for the whole of Andrew Ford's hour-long program. Getting older, music taste for melodies from the early 20th century, and why not? (And I actually listened to the repeat of Andrew Ford's program several months later, 11.05pm to midnight.)

Dear *All That Jazz*,

I hope you won't be too affronted when I tell you that when I first saw you, I experienced quite some distaste and dislike. I'm not sure why now. I had expected to like you very much – a film by, and something of a portrait of, dancer and choreographer, Bob Fosse. I don't know what persuaded me to go and see you again, but I did – and the result was something of a 180° turn in my response.

Perhaps I will realise a little better why by the time I finish this letter to you. And I should add that I have watched you again just recently, impressed, over forty years since I saw you those first two times.

One of the main reasons for wanting to see you in 1979 was memories of Bob Fosse himself, seeing him as a dancer, especially in *Kiss Me Kate*, small but immediately noticeable, and his sleek and sinuous dancing style. After directing shows on Broadway, he had also moved into film direction in 1969 with *Sweet Charity* and I admired him very much when he won an Oscar as best director in 1972 for *Cabaret*. Now here he was, actor, dancer, choreographer, director, co-writing and directing you, a show about putting on a show on Broadway.

Semi-autobiographical, you focus on Fosse's obsession with dancing, his inability to form permanent relationships, his womanising, his workaholism, his disregard of his health and reliance on drugs.

You are highly imaginative, blending a realistic look at putting on a show but a fantasy framework where the dying Joe Gideon (Roy Scheider in one of his best performances) reviews his life in an offhand way, discussing it with the Angel of Death, a strangely elaborately-dressed Jessica Lange. You also show his relationship with his wife, Gwen Verdon, played by dancer Leland Palmer, another love of his life, played by dancer Ann Reinking (really playing herself and her dancing and personal partnership with Fosse).

In the meantime, you show us Fosse editing one of his films, *The Stand-Up*, which gives comedian, Cliff Gorman, the opportunity to do some stand-up comedy routines about Elizabeth Kubler-Ross's Five Stages of Death – which then Joe Gideon has to apply to himself. And he does in a blend of the offhand and the cynical.

Because the show must go on, you have many rehearsal sequences, the musical numbers have the characteristically sinuous and rhythmic style of Fosse's choreography, especially the opening audition number and the Air-otic sequence which brings sexuality and sensuality to a song about people going on board a plane. You are also very stylised with Ben Vereen doing the dancing in the final parody of 'Bye Bye Love' as 'Bye Bye Life' while Joe Gideon dies. As well there are some entertaining numbers with Ann Reinking and Leland Palmer, especially 'Everything Old is New Again'.

Plenty to enjoy and admire.

You also show the life behind the scenes, the financial deals, the rivalry amongst directors and producers so that there is realistic background to the hard work and glamour of the Broadway production show.

I should tell you that while I was writing this letter to you, I was also remembering watching the television series last year, *Fosse/Verdon*. Sam Rockwell was no more sympathetic than Roy Scheider – how much self-loathing was there in Fosse's own life? But Michelle Williams brought Gwen Verdon sympathetically to life.

A lot of the reflections that I have written in this letter to you come from the eventual review I wrote at the time, the favourable response. We see the face of show business but you take us behind the face, behind the facade, inviting us into the depths.

Dear *The Last Temptation of Christ*,

That is not exactly the way you were spoken to or spoken of towards the end of 1988. In fact, you were far from dear to many outraged Christians (without the benefit of having seen you) who became militant. I always remember that protesters in 1500 cars travelled to Universal Studios in Los Angeles to demand that the president of the company destroy your negative (and paid for parking in the Universal lot, Universal making a profit – at least $1500, I suppose, minimum – from the venture). In Australia, we kept reading about the condemnations, the insult to the person of Jesus Christ, the blasphemous nature of the film...

Before telling you what effect you had on me as a reviewer, I would like to affirm how much I appreciated, and still appreciate, you. It was interesting to note before seeing you, that you are based on a novel, rather than specifically on the Gospels as such (which many of your critics assumed). It was even more interesting to note that novelist, Nikos Kazantzakis, a member of the Greek Orthodox Church, was actually excommunicated. And then, your screenplay was written by that stern Michigan-born Calvinist, Paul Schrader (remembering *Taxi Driver*) and directed by New York Italian Catholic, Martin Scorsese (and remembering now images of blood, Jesus reaching into his chest and pulling out his heart, the Sacred Heart, or the apostles at the Last Supper, biting into the bread and blood flowing down their lips and chins).

But writer and filmmakers were exploring the continual mystery of the Incarnation, that Jesus was fully human, that Jesus, one with the Father, was divine. And the perennial questions, how can that be, what are the consequences, how much do we appreciate the humanity, how much are we aware of the divinity? In the one person? You wanted to put the emphasis on this human nature/divine nature struggle in Jesus himself, in the human condition and its limitations, of suffering, death, and choices to be made.

In fact – at least here in Australia – a large part of your audience consisted of theology students, interested in exploring these issues.

Because of the American campaigns, the Australian chief censor at the time, John Dickie, prudently invited representatives of all the churches to pre-release previews. I was one of the representatives from Victoria. You may remember that none of the representatives considered you blasphemous except the leader of the Festival of Light, parliamentarian, Fred Nile. But the Premier of Queensland, Joh Bjelke Petersen, decided that you should have an R 18+ certificate rather than the M 15+, as in the other states.

In Melbourne, a group of us were invited by the evening newspaper, the *Herald*, to a roundtable discussion to provide feature for the paper. The first person to speak was television personality, devout Catholic, Bert Newton, who seemed to feel a bit trapped, that he ought to be negative about you. When a member of the National Civic Council, a Right-Leaning group, stated that he had seen the original screenplay, that there were overtones of homosexuality in the kiss that John the Baptist gave Jesus after the baptism, Terry Lane, ABC broadcaster, from the Churches of Christ, reacted strongly reminding us that the last temptation was not about sexuality but to give up on one's destiny.

The discussion was stimulating, my contribution was to comment about how the screenplay and treatment dramatised well the Gospel narratives and the themes, linking with the Old Testament writings. Not particularly controversial.

However, the ABC rang to ask whether I would be prepared to engage in a discussion on ABC Gippsland with the local member of the House of Representatives, National Party Catholic, Peter McGauran. I still have the tape – the temptation to listen to it again! He told the listeners that he certainly was not going to see the film. He declared that I was the type of priest who was emptying the churches these days. When I tried to venture a comment about

Jesus' human nature and his divine nature, Peter McGauran batted me off by declaring that he was a simple Catholic. The producer came on the phone to tell me that with the talkback, nobody was supporting what I had said. So that was it.

Well, not quite, Gippsland members of the Catholic Women's League wrote protests to my community leader as well as to the provincial superior, aggressive letters (putting charity aside). Both the superiors, in fact, without my knowing it, responded to all these letters confirming that I was in good standing, theologically, and as a priest.

The controversy passed, though it remains in the people's memories. However, over the years, I have used you or used clips in seminars and, often, members of the group stimulated by the clips have wanted to watch you in full.

I don't know whether you remember that there were protests in Melbourne outside the Russell Centre by members of a fringe group of the Greek Orthodox community, carrying placards, not always correct spelling. The manager of the cinemas was naturally upset, especially when they used the toilets during the protest. However, he was pacified somewhat because, when they were hungry, they frequented the candy bar. And, you might remember the protester with the placard amongst the Greeks outside the Sydney Pitt Centre with his placard: 'this film is blasphemous. Brian is the Messiah'. It's a wonder this member of the Monty Python club survived!

So strange memories, but some very good memories, and appreciation of your initiative in dramatising spiritual and theological issues.

Dear *Witness Protection*,

I had no idea when I pressed the play button one Sunday night during our Melbourne Stage 4 coronavirus lockdown that I would be writing a letter to you. But somewhere near halfway through, realising I was becoming very involved, it seemed a good idea and that stayed with me until the final credits.

I see your date is 1999, an HBO production, but I was not aware of you at all but you looked as if you had an interesting cast and Witness Protection is often an interesting dramatic theme. Well, that is an understatement from me in your regard!

One of the main things that struck me as I watched your drama unfolding is that I really didn't know very much about the Witness Protection process at all. Like many audiences, I presume, we simply thought that individuals and families in danger were told to change their identities and some American government office organised their move to a city on the other side of the country – and so it is, in your case, from Boston to Seattle. But as regards any details, preparation, the suddenness of the transition, awareness of difficulties, they had not really occurred to me. Well, you certainly brought home some powerfully critical issues.

One of the challenges is that the central character, Bob 'Batts' Batton, played so convincingly by Tom Sizemore, is a thug, practically no redeeming features except love for his wife (and certainly not 100% on that) and concern for his children though he was often an absentee father, never going to school meetings or his son's debates. After an attempt on his life in his home, he is pressurised by the FBI to give testimony against his boss. Reluctant, he does record his testimony for court use and, fearing for his life and for his family, he does not give much thought as to what entering the Witness Protection program would entail. Nor did I.

But the bulk of your action shows the family travelling to an isolated and secure facility, supervised by Forest Whitaker (in yet another of his sympathetic but strong-minded roles), five days of quite intense training, rethinking, challenge to adaptation, and presentation of the realities of living in the program. They are not going to be supported by taxpayers' money (which, perhaps, I had thought they were), Bob, now becoming Bill Cooper, has to find a job and is not qualified and has no references or experience. His financial situation was crooked and, even with the selling of his house and cars, the family is bankrupt. He and his wife will both have to work. The little daughter is five and, while she is persuaded that they have to play pretend so that the bad man will not find them, she is caught up in the moods of the family. The son, a good performance by Shawn Hatosy, is a teenager, losing his friends, losing his school, losing his achievements, at one stage determined to get out and return to Boston despite the risks.

So you present a most demanding learning experience for the unprepared family as well as quite an absorbing and challenging learning experience for us, the audience.

The second stream running through is that of the interactions of the family. Bob is certainly not an ideal husband and father, used to bossing people around, used to luxury in his life. He is not an easy learner, often disruptive, becoming more and more moody, snapping at his daughter, but a huge confrontation with his son, his son rebelling, no holds barred and a swing back, and an even more dramatic and powerful confrontation with his wife, even to physical violence, on her part. I was profoundly moved, sometimes shocked at these revelations and the repercussions, regretting that Cindy had gone along with her husband in the past, somewhat overwhelmed with her in her discovering their financial situation and prospects in Seattle. This portrait of Cindy brings home the complexities and subtleties of hers and the family situation. I think it is the best performance I have seen from Mary Elizabeth Mastrantonio.

So your screenplay contains powerful sequences about family interactions, tense, sometimes hyper-tense, of a man caught in the consequences of his own irresponsible and selfish actions, but the overwhelming consequences for his wife and children – so much discovering the strain of continual alertness, dissembling, deceiving, deflecting, evading, non-comittalling.

Thank you for being such an effective film made for television, for a strong screenplay, for a talented director, Richard Pearce, a number of whose thrillers I have very much liked. Thanks, indeed, for opening up some worlds so distant from my own.

Dear *The Tree of Life*,

I have to confess to you that I did not respond well to you back in 2011. However, a long-ago student of mine wrote, expecting that I would have a letter to you in this collection. I had not intended it but, urged on by some of his comments and questions, I thought I should check what I wrote in review at the time of your release. Looking at it, I realise that you had been provocative and that I had responded with more thought than I remembered.

So, here you are, a letter to a movie that did not appeal to me. Whether one likes you or not – and right from Cannes 2011 where critics split into both camps but the International Jury awarded you the Palme D' Or – I have to admit that you are ambitious in content and scope.

Those in favour see you as creative in ideas and cinema storytelling. Those not in favour prefer to see you as pretentious. But one person's pretentions are another's earnestness.

With Kubrick's 1968 *2001: A Space Odyssey*, which many quote in comparison, I found it immediately overwhelming. I didn't find you overwhelming, but there was a great deal to respond to and to reflect on.

In recent years, I have appreciated *To the Wonder* and *A Hidden Life*. With you Terrence Malick uses poetic realism in his narrative about an average American family and special effects in his cosmological and biological portrait of the evolving world as well as a visit to a surprising land of life after death.

Who could resist an opening quotation from the Book of Job, chapter 38? The Job allusions would repay study. They are a challenge to humans in the face of the reality of God, creation and the sustaining of the universe. Who are we really? How do we compare with God? I wonder did Malick go to Job 42: 1-5. It contains the answer to Malick's initial quotation. It is a profoundly humble acknowledgment of human empty-headed words in the face of the mystery of God. Job must be silent in the face of God's grandeur and majesty.

Malick then follows this with comments on nature and grace. He states that nature can be competitive and destructive whereas grace offers a spirituality of humility, honesty and integrity and respect and regard for others. This is important for his portrait of the family.

As regards the universe, there is much to admire in his visualising of what looks like an interpretation of the Big Bang or a Creative Theophany. The dinosaurs make an impression. The changing earth looks cosmically arresting.

Malick does not quite begin with the cosmology. It comes after our introduction to a family, the O' Briens in the 1950s, and so there is a jolt as we are taken back into prehistory. Once Malick establishes that our world has evolved – here we are.

The first episode in the life of the family is the news of the death of a son in war, the delivery of the sad telegram to the mother and the grief of the father. In a way, or in many ways, the story of the family is particularly ordinary. There is a value in our seeing the average family. There is a disadvantage insofar as this is not so engagingly dramatic.

The mother (Jessica Chastain) is a fine and beautiful woman, devoted to her husband until she has to face the challenge of his changing and his frustrations and the sometimes erratic treatment of his three sons. She seems the personification of Malick's grace. The father is basically a good man who can face the reality of his failings and can apologise. He also lives through life's ups and downs, his family growing up, his work achievements, humiliation in unemployment. This is an interesting role for Brad Pitt as he nears fifty, not a glamorous or celebrity role but rather an embodiment of the American male who is a personification of nature with moments of grace.

Actually, the real focus of the film is the oldest son. He is played with quite some intense hostility by first-timer, Hunter McCracken.

Whatever it is in McCracken's face and eyes, I became mesmerised by him and his struggles with his love for and dislike of his father, a father who is torn by his strong-willed discipline which cowers his son and his deep-seated but too often unexpressed love. We see a lot of Jack and even viscerally share his tormented transition from young boy to teenager. Many of these scenes are with his brothers, the younger the one who is to die, the littlest just hanging in there.

This is not a particularly interesting family in itself or in what it does, but it can be seen as a typical, even archetypal average American family.

Since Malick does not seem to need narrative order, accuracy or coherence, we move in and out of flashforwards, to Jack as a middle-aged adult, working in skyscraper offices, puzzled by life and in a context which seems loomingly apocalyptic. So this is how Jack turned out. And he is portrayed by a time-ravaged Sean Penn.

Since Malick has shown us his interpretation of the past, the recent past and the present, he then ventures into the future.

His afterlife is symbolic (we hope), people wandering an empty landscape, bypassing each other, but many connecting. It is hard to portray an afterlife on screen. Film-makers often opt for what seems a purgatorial state or experience, a prelude to what we might hope is heaven, an In-Between. Father and mother and the children arrive, wander, but are reunited with the adult Jack. It would seem that our lives and our after-lives are times of grace.

The Tree of Life (and there is a symbolic tree at the family home) is a religious film in the broadest sense. It would be interesting to hear an atheist's interpretation, probably dismissal of these spiritual dimensions except in so far as they are the aspirations of most humans whether they are fulfilled or not. For the believer in the broadest sense (which includes the agnostic who does not disbelieve but claims that we cannot know God), there are many of what Peter Berger called 'signals of transcendence'. Malick avoids much explicit connection to religion, but he is showing us a basically Christian culture, with reference to Job and the language of grace.

Christians can well appreciate his attempt to portray this religious perspective. After all St Thomas Aquinas, following the arguments of Aristotle, for a basic mover, cause and imaginer of the universe, acknowledges that people express this belief in their own ways. But he adds, for the Christian, this source of all being, we call 'God'. I was surprised to reread how much I had written about you and the trouble I seemed to have taken to give serious consideration what you are communicating. So I have turned it into a letter to you – and, as you would guess, my conclusion is that I should give serious thought to watching you again.

Dear *Enola Holmes*,

This is a letter to you. But, through you, a greeting to Enola Holmes herself, a young woman I would like to meet. And, I would like to tell her how much I enjoyed Millie Bobby Brown's bringing her to life, so vivacious, so strong, so enterprising.

In fact, I started my review by stating that I found you a delight. In fact, I found you a treat. I suppose this is where some confession comes up concerning Arthur Conan Doyle and Sherlock Holmes.

Like everyone, I suppose, I am always very happy to be immersed in Sherlock's world. I can't remember how I was introduced – probably via reading Conan Doyle's novels, one of the earliest memories being *The Hound of the Baskervilles*. And there have been so many cinema incarnations of Sherlock, the strict intensity of Basil Rathbone, contrasting with the cheeky bravado of Robert Downey, classic Christopher Lee and Peter Cushing, television's Jeremy Brett, the eccentric aristocracy of Benedict Cumberbatch and, my favourite, Ian Richardson (perfect in *The Sign of Four*). Actually, one of my favourites is *Without a Trace*, the comedy where Michael Caine portrays the bumbling Sherlock who is a front for Ben Kingsley's Dr Watson doing all the solving. And the invention of Sigerson Holmes, Gene Wilder as Sherlock Holmes' smarter brother. I have also enjoyed very much going back to the *Young Sherlock Holmes* and relishing Ian McKellen as the older, retired *Mr Holmes*. Well, perhaps the Conan Doyle purists may not be so tolerant of all these imaginings – but most of us are.

I don't know whether you enjoyed all those reminiscences but I certainly enjoyed naming them and remembering them.

And so you present us with Sherlock's and Mycroft's younger sister. Father dead, the older brothers left home long since, Enola at home with her mother, Helena Bonham Carter, obviously a suffragette before her time, the widow who takes active pleasure in training her daughter in all kinds of fields, reading and history, science and engineering, delighting in codes and words, anagrams and advanced scrabble techniques, Enola defending herself, taking initiatives, all seen in many enjoyable intercut flashbacks. (I had been wondering about the name, Enola, memories of the atomic bomb on Hiroshima, Enola Gay, But back to the codes, Enola being an anagram of Alone!).

One of your great strengths, of course, is the casting. Millie Bobby Brown makes quite an impression as the 16-year-old Enola. Those encountering Millie Bobby Brown for the first time might think that she has quite a future ahead of her – only to find that she has an extensive past in both film and television, especially *Stranger Things*. She is a vital and dynamic screen presence and the screenplay provides her with wonderful opportunities to look straight to camera, to make comments, to raise eyebrows, to engage us in all her moods, her aspirations, sharers in all her plans and activities. I would have liked even more of her confiding in us.

And well we might ask, where is Sherlock? And to a lesser interest and extent, where is Mycroft? They have long since left home, Mycroft in business, politically conservative (to say the least), enjoying his club, but, with the disappearance of their mother, Enola becoming his ward. Sherlock has already made his mark in the world of detection. Sam Claflin plays Mycroft, communicating his insufferability. Sherlock is played by Henry Cavill. (This reviewer always has problems with Henry Cavill, usually giving rather stolid performances, even as Superman, more suited to Clark Kent – although he has the looks of the genial Christopher Reeve.)

Yes, I enjoyed very much the adventure, the detection, Sherlock involved, of course, but Enola discovering and developing her talent. It concerns a young lord, the Marquis of Tewkesbury (Louis Partridge), a soft-looking youth – with Enola remarking that he is looking like the nincompoop he was born to be! (Yes, she does have a way with words.) The mystery involves the death of his father, a seemingly menacing uncle, his detached mother, his strong dowager grandmother, and a sadistic assassin with a bowler hat. And it is the time for votes in the House of Lords, for women's rights, for women's demonstrations (including stashes of gunpowder).

And there are some wonderful cameos. Helena Bonham Carter, always distinctive, Fiona Shaw the bombastic headmistress of the school for ladies and proper manners (but with some heart flutters for Mycroft), Frances de la Tour is the dowager, Burn Gorman is the assassin. I noticed that throughout the film ethnic groups are represented in London, Inspector Lestrade (Adeel Akhtar with Pakistani father, Kenyan mother; cafe owner and martial arts instructor, Edith (Susan Mokowa, Nigerian parents) and a number of incidental characters played by West Indians and Asian actors.)

Talking of sensibilities – you are based on a Young Adult novel by Nancy Springer – though, interestingly, your screenplay is written by Jack Thorne and directed by Harry Bradbeer.

I ended my review with some advice – surrender to the Holmes family, their adventures, and the atmosphere of 19th-century London and country estates. A treat.

Dear *The Devil all the Time*,

It seemed best to begin my review with a caution: 'Just in case someone looking at the title thinks that it is light, even flippant title, beware. This is quite a serious piece of Americana, taking us back to the end of World War II and the beginnings of the war in Vietnam, 1945-1965'.

I thought I should add that, the Devil receives only one explicit mention, one of the preachers giving a homily about Jesus and his being tested by the devil. The Devil is a tester and an accuser. However, by contrast, you have many mentions of God, quite a lot of God language.

I did have an opportunity to visit West Virginia (to Harper's Ferry and Civil war memories, John Brown, the Potomac and the Shenandoah). It seemed a long way away from Virginia – and always intriguing in movies which take us to what seem to be the backblocks. While your main settings are in West Virginia and adjacent parts of Ohio, somewhat isolated in those years, you actually open in the South Pacific, a group of soldiers on patrol, suddenly confronted by one of their fellow GIs impaled on a cross, bleeding and tortured, a jolting experience for them as well as for us. No missing the symbol. But, it sets something of a tone about good and evil, about God and suffering, the cross and prayer, faith and loss of faith.

I found myself identifying with the GI, Willard, Bill Skarsgaard, affected by the experience, returning home, and encountering at a diner a kindly waitress giving food to a derelict man. After getting home, greeting his mother, a very religious woman, a churchgoer, he returns to the diner and marries the waitress. They have a young boy. Willard recovers his faith, goes into the woods where he has planted a cross, sometimes praying desperately, eventually commanding his young son to pray, especially when his wife, the boy's mother, has terminal cancer. Very emotionally involving.

While initially you focus on Willard and his son, who will grow up to be at the centre of your later drama, you draw us into several other narrative strands throwing different light on life in West Virginia, one strand religious, the other strand secular and immoral. In fact, of the principal characters, six are murdered and two commit suicide. But the thing is that most of these take place in a religious context.

We realise that religious communities at this time in West Virginia and Ohio were evangelical, small local communities, a local preacher, reliance on sermons, prayer, strong prayer of petition, a basic faith in Jesus. (There is not the kind of fundamentalist assertion of faith and beliefs that is more commonly found in these churches in the 21st-century.) But you challenge a contemporary audience to think about faith, the impact of genuine faith, delusions of messianic faith, the hypocrisy of faith as a context for violence and sexual abuse.

Willard loses his faith with his wife's cancer. His son inherits no faith though accompanies his grandmother to church. One of the early alarming characters is a self-proclaimed preacher and mesmeric healer, Roy – Harry Melling in a sinister and frightening performance, who marries a young woman in the town, Mia Wasikowska, and they have a daughter. However, Roy believes that God will answer all his prayers – even to his killing someone and praying in desperate belief that they will resurrect. At this stage, you are definitely alarming. And he meets a sad and brutal fate.

In the next generation, in the 1960s, the local preacher, ailing, invites a younger man from Tennessee to take over the parish, suave, presentable, talking the language of faith, claiming integrity and leadership. His played by Robert Pattinson. It is he who is the hypocrite, religiously seductive, ultimately a coward in the face of a challenge to his beliefs and behaviour. And the challenge comes from Willard's son, played by Tom Holland.

The secular strand in your story turns out to be a disgusting one, serial killers, killers for sexual thrills, photographing their victims, caught up in some local electioneering for the sheriff – illustrating, certainly, the devil all the time in their lives.

Ultimately, you bring all the strands together.

One of the surprises is the realisation that the actors portraying Americans in this area and period, three British, two Australian, one Swedish, one of Romanian origins – certainly an international mixum gatherum of performers in American cinema.

One of your principal interesting features is that you are narrated by the author of the original novel, Donald Ray Pollock. He is able to make commentary on all the characters, on the situations, to do a lot of the explicit moralising.

You offer us a frightening and pessimistic collection of moral fables.

Dear *Phone Booth*,

I hope a good number of people have seen you. At one stage in my work, you were quite significant for seminars on films and values. In fact, when preparing *Lights..., Camera..., Faith... The 10 Commandments*, you were an immediate choice to illustrate the eighth commandment on lying.

One of the immediate attractions to you was your director, Joel Schumacher, his films usually bright and colourful (after all, he was a costume and production designer), two Grisham adaptations, two Batman films, *The Phantom of the Opera*... He makes a phone booth in central Manhattan look good. And, you were written by Larry Cohen, whose films were generally intriguing, small-budget horror films with a moral message (*It's Alive, Q-the Winged Serpent*, for instance). So, you see, I was pre-disposed to like you.

Your central character, Stu Shephard (Colin Farrell, always an interesting screen presence) is an Everyman figure. Admittedly, he is a pretty low-grade Everyman. For starters, he is a publicist, not a shrinking violet, rather more in your face with his promotions. His deals for clients define who he is – his clothes, mobile phone, also help in the definition. He does not walk. He does not amble. He struts. He does love his wife in his way, but he is not averse to using a phone box, removing his wedding ring, to phone a girlfriend.

One day, his visit turns into a life-challenging, life-changing experience. I've mentioned to you that you come across as a moral fable. It was sometimes said in the past that the phone booth was something like a confessional. And, with you, it certainly is – and more. It is a life and death experience.

In saying life and death experience, I wanted to say that Stu has something of a purgatorial experience. Which takes me to a theological book by our student director back in the day, Jim Cuskelly. It had two titles, one for Americans. *God's Gracious Design*. The other, for the rest of us, was *The Kindness of God*. I like them both. Jim wrote about the death experience, something which has always remained with me. His description of death was not of our simply going unconscious, then stepping into heaven or hell or, the interim experience of cleansing one's soul, purgatory.

He suggested we step out of time into God's dimension, experiencing our judgment at once, so to speak, our affirming our God-commitment – in the presence of God, realising and acknowledging (honest to God) our failures, our sinfulness, repenting and being purged. (And I have always hoped that this is the experience of everyone, even the most loathsome and atrocious sinner in this life -no need for hell!)

And this, it seems to me, is what happens in your screenplay. Stu answers the phone. He is told not to hang up. He is threatened with death. The anonymous speaker lists Stu's sins, his superficial life and deals, his vanity, the betrayal of his wife, the compromising of his girlfriend... Your running time is brief, 88 minutes, but you compel us to share something of Stu's being caught up in what seems to be an infinity of time. The accused. The accuser. The initial dishonest response, gradual admission of the truth, an overpowering sense of guilt, the need for forgiveness and redemption.

I've simplified this a bit – after all, the crowd gathers, the sympathetic policeman arrives, Forest Whitaker (who is forced into some truth admissions himself). His wife arrives and Stu has to acknowledge the truth. The girlfriend is present. And there is the media as well as a crowd of onlookers. Something of a public judgment.

In the *God's Gracious Design* scenario, we have to face the truth of God. (There is a Psalm which says 'in your light, we see light'). But the accuser in your scenario seems diabolical. He boasts to Stu that he has executed several men morally guilty of cruelty, greed, or deception, who would not confess to their sins and failings. The accuser is hellish.

(Which reminded me that decades ago, Clint Eastwood did the same kind of ambiguity of accusation and condemnation as the *High Plains Drifter*, coming to the reckless town, Jesus-like saving the widows, the orphans, the poor, but coming back at night, trapping the evil (men), painting the town red, setting it alight, and placing a notice 'Hell', the town by the burning lake.)

By the way, for *Lights..., Camera..., Faith...*, I had to pick some biblical references for discussion about your meaning. What came to mind was the Adam and Eve story in Genesis 3, the couple's succumbing to the tempter, a confession experience, stripped literally and morally naked before God. And then, in the Gospels, there was the story of Peter, a boaster, presumptuous, tested, denying Jesus, accused, weeping. But, not to forget Jesus' rehabilitation of him, asking him to acknowledge his love, commissioning him as a leader.

Who knows what happened to Stu after this phone booth confessional experience? Something – or a lot more – for the better, we hope.

Many thanks for showing how a movie can be an effective moral fable.

Dear *Crocodile Dundee*,

G'day. In 1986, that's probably how most Australians would have greeted you. Actually, I'm probably mistaken – that we would have said G'day *Crocodile Dundee*. We all went to see you and thoroughly enjoyed the experience. We appreciated a good laugh. We were forced to have a look at ourselves. In fact, there were a lot of serious themes underlying the comedy, thinking of Aboriginal issues and Australian history, thinking of the environment, thinking of the myths we have created about ourselves and which need some debunking.

And good on Paul Hogan. He had been part of our awareness for more than a decade, his comedy skits on television, working on the Harbour Bridge, deadpan situations, larrikin one-liners. And back in those days when people smoked, he was part of our consciousness whether we smoked or not and gave the word 'anyhow' more status and popularity than anyone would have with unexpected placements: 'Anyhow, have a Winfield!'

Whatever reservations some members of society had about Paul Hogan and his image, most of them disappeared when you were screened.

So, safari in the Northern Territory, flora and fauna, mesmerising buffalo, outback pubs, Aboriginal icon, David Gulpilil, in trousers and paint, and Mick Dundee as guide, opening up the Northern Territory where most Australians had not yet ventured but were beginning to make travel plans.

In your own way, your characters, situations, quips and comments were offering something of a pleasing, if distortedly questioning, mirror for our reflection.

There was a theme in literature, the innocent abroad. It usually referred to Americans let loose in Europe, sometimes insensitive, trampling through the old traditions, on a learning expedition. With your shift in screenplay from the Northern Territory to New York City, Mick Dundee became the innocent Australian abroad, really unaware of how the United States ticks, making all kind of blunders, but bringing his naive kindness to people on the margins.

And who would have thought a simple line like 'now that's a knife' would become part of our vocabulary – facing the muggers with their knives and pulling out his blade with triumphant satisfaction? On the other hand, he had to face the issue of where you wash your underwear and hang it out to dry!

There have been documentaries about Paul Hogan, and a television miniseries about his life, its ups and downs, his marrying Linda Kozlowski, tax problems, moves between the US and Australia, and regrettable facelifts. Whatever those difficulties may be, they are not part of the unanticipated and powerful impact you made in 1986.

There are lots of anecdotes in you so I'll take the opportunity to add my own *Crocodile Dundee* anecdote. It involves the justice-campaigning American Jesuit, Father Daniel Berrigan. He was a guest in 1986 at the National Pastoral Institute where I was a member of the staff. He was a most impressive man, fitting in with ease, talking happily about Jesuit community life after the Second Vatican Council, but talking about his eventful life, dramatic protests, court cases, prison, only when asked. He gave a recital of his poetry at the Melbourne Arts Centre with conservative be-furred Catholics demonstrating outside. I remember controversial broadcaster, Derryn Hinch, came out from his studio to the foyer to welcome Dan Berrigan.

And, yes, we took him to see you at the Hoyts Cinema Centre. He enjoyed the experience thoroughly – while asking some questions of clarification about Australianisms. But the point of this anecdote is that six months later, we received a letter from him (which I still have in a folder) where he thanked us because he was able to take a very sick Jesuit confrere in New York City to see you, cheering him up immensely. (So that's my claim to fame in having influenced Daniel Berrigan!)

And I find I am smiling as I write this appreciative letter to you.

Dear *Jo-Jo Rabbit*,

This is going to be a warmer letter to you than I might have written twenty years ago. The beginning of the explanation is this. I used to be very happy, enjoying mimicking the New Ziland iccent. Not that New Zealanders don't mimic the Australian accent!

I always enjoyed quoting the sketch in the 1990s television *Fast Forward* featuring the New Zealand Dubbing Association, the members all dressed and looking like novelist Janet Frame from *An Angel at My Table*. When asked if dubbing was necessary in New Zealand, Magda Szubanski spoke up, quoting the last line of Casablanca: 'Thus could be the begunning of a beautiful frundshup'. (Actually, I had troubles of my own while celebrating Mass, particularly at the doxology where, it seems, the New Zealand congregation heard me pray: 'Weeth heem, een heem, through heem, een the uneety of the Holy Speereet...'. While I heard them pray: 'Wuth hum, un hum, through hum, un the unuty of the Holy Spurut...'.)

Our family had always believed that our maternal grandfather was born in Scotland and had migrated to New Zealand before moving to Sydney. In applying for a UK visa, the information came back that the same grandfather was not only born in Dunedin, he lived there for 37 years before coming to Australia. A New Zealand grandfather!! Suddenly, I began praising *The Piano* and *Lord of the Rings*!

Which is all the preamble to praising your director, Taika Waititi, not only a New Zealander but with both Maori and Jewish background. Which, of course, stands him in good stead in tackling your story of a 10-year-old boy in Germany, member of the Hitler youth, caught up in the complexities of World War II. Taika Waititi has shown over the years what a different sense of humour he has.

Who else would have vampires taking refuge in a boarding house in Antipodean Wellington, *What We Do in the Shadows*? And he has a way with engaging the audience with stories of boys, *Boy* and the laconic Julian Denison roughing it with gruff South Islander, Sam Neill, in *The Hunt for the Wilderpeople*.

He also capitalised on his New Ziland accent as the Stone King, Korg, in *Thor Ragnorak* (which he directed). And, here he is Hitler.

It was Aristotle who said there was catharsis in drama and in comedy. Did he say that there was catharsis in parody? If there is, and audiences need some catharsis because of memories of the Holocaust, then you are in a strong tradition. After all, at the beginning of World War II, Charlie Chaplin mimicked Hitler in *The Great Dictator*. After all, hadn't Hitler paid Chaplin the compliment of mimicking his moustache! And what about Mel Brooks and *The Producers* with the musical spectacular, 'Springtime for Hitler in Germany'!

A telling cinema reference would be *Cabaret* with the close-up of the enthusiastic, angelic looking boy singing so earnestly and the camera drawing back to reveal him as a member of the Hitler Youth.

You help us follow Jo Jo in his Hitler youth training, an officer forcing him to kill a rabbit, which he could not, hence his nickname, Rebel Wilson and her urging the boys to burn books, and the tall, gaunt Stephen Merchant turning up, dressed in black, arriving with his henchmen, parody repetitions of Heil Hitler on first arrival, then on the arrival of the military captain, then with the emergence of Elsa into the room. Heil Hitlering has never looked so idiotic!

And, of course, the presence of Hitler himself. Young boys often have imaginary friends so, in the atmosphere of the Third Reich, what more appropriate than Jo to have Hitler. But his Hitler acts like a 10-year-old, cheerful, moody, petulant, erratic, giving Nazi advice, peddling the ideology, a child in an adult Hitler body. It is a tour de force performance.

However, your screenplay has many serious themes running through it, the young girl hidden in the house, Jo Jo's emotional dilemma, and, especially, JoJo's relationship with his mother – with some brutal pathos.

And, as you near your end, we wonder what the resolution could possibly be. How much will be dramatic and sad? How much will be funny and parody? You answer the question marvellously with Hitler overreaching himself with his friend and JoJo left with nothing else but to boot him out the window!

How much we enjoy the defenestration of Hitler!

Dear *The Pawnbroker*,

I am writing to tell you about the two shocks I had when I first saw you in a small arthouse cinema in Sydney in the latter part of 1966. One was a long-term shock. The other was a short-term shock.

I would like to go with the long-term shock first. It concerns the Holocaust. In Australia, memory tells me that we were sheltered from information about the Holocaust. I was six when the war in Europe ended and have no memory of it. Then, especially with the movies at school, we saw a lot of those British war movies, *The Wooden Horse*, *The Colditz Story*, *Above Us the Waves*... – quite a lot of them, and I think we were permeated with ra-ra British patriotism. The German characters like Marius Goring snarling, were villains (if not caricatures). Unfortunately, I was in the seminary studying philosophy when *The Diary of Anne Frank* was released in 1959. So at least I must have had some kind of awareness of the Nazi treatment of Jews, the transfer to the concentration camps, the ovens.

I have just remembered that a popular book in the late 1950s was called *The Victory of Father Karl* (who was interned in Dachau) and that during the ceremony of our making our first vows, our Provincial Superior, Father Kerrins, used the book for his homily with reference to our profession and self-commitment.

As I was coming back home from Rome studies in 1966, I had a short stopover in Munich and one of the things that I wanted to do was to visit Dachau, memories of Fr Karl. As I remember, there were no signs from the Dachau station as to the direction of the camp. I asked directions, and had a longish walk. Now that I think of it, it was only twenty-one years since the end of the war, the opening up of the camps. I have only vague memories now but

I do remember the rows of huts, their extent, and trying to imagine what the internment was like.

Which is rather a long introduction to telling you about my first shock. It was how you showed the Holocaust survivors living in New York City, and flashbacks, of course, to life in the camps, and death in the camps. In one sense, many of those survivors, like Rod Steiger's pawnbroker, were the walking dead, living on in body, the pathos of memories and lost memories, bitterness, much hopelessness, and caught up in the harsh and immoral jungles of the American city. Living still but dispirited (unspirited) survival. And is the pawnbroker another incarnation of 'the wandering Jew'?

We have learnt so much since the 1960s, information, books, movies – and the mystery of Holocaust denial. (In 1994, in Poland, I chose to visit Auschwitz, overwhelming – how can anyone deny!)

For something of the emotional impact, I want to include some words that I wrote to *Schindler's List*:

> At the press preview in the Paramount Theatrette, I found myself sitting next to one of the survivors and his wife. And then, he became one of the characters. And the most moving moment for me, bringing home the reality, that final sequence where your characters, accompanied by the real-life survivors, including the man sitting next to me, were filmed placing stones on the grave of the righteous Oskar Schindler in Jerusalem. That memory is at this moment coming back to me emotionally and I hear the strains of John Williams' plaintive score, its sadness and lament.

If you remember the comment at the time about one of your scenes which achieved a certain notoriety, a woman briefly baring her breasts, you will not be surprised to know that that was the second, the short-term, shock. As I look back over many decades of bare breasts and beyond, it is surprising to realise that we were so shocked. I can't remember that I had seen bare breasts on screen before that time.

Your scene was highly significant for a change in American Catholic perspectives on what could be seen on screen or what should be censored. A remark was made at the time that if this scene were not cut, you would open the floodgates. That, in retrospect, seems like an understatement! However, in the tradition of the American Catholic Legion of Decency, established in 1934, with strict classifications, including C for condemned, and Catholics asked to make a pledge to abide by these classifications, you received a C.

There had been some criticisms and controversy in the 1950s concerning the Motion Picture Code and the Legion – Otto Preminger's *The Moon is Blue* being condemned for actually including a screenplay the words 'virgin' and 'pregnant'. Moira Walsh, a Catholic critic of the time, stated that your C classification did not do justice to you, did not indicate your quality as a film, the desperate intensity and humanity challenge of your themes. So you were one of the contributors to the demise of the Legion and the development of more helpful classification and information and advice (although the official Catholic reviews through the Catholic News Service still tend to narrow interpretations, almost nit-picking objections in terms of sexuality, language, violence and the ever-frequent categorising, 'Morally Offensive').

I began writing on films by 1965, regularly reviewing from the beginning of 1968, remembering my response to your notorious scene, realising that to ask about 'what is presented' can be a narrowing perspective, because all human activity can be the subject of storytelling and the arts (just thinking of all the category of sinfulness in the Old Testament!). The real question to be asking is 'how is it presented' and the interplay between sensitivity and morality.

But that sounds as if I'm preparing notes for a workshop so I'll simply finish by saying thank you for that 1966 alert to the impact of the Holocaust and the consequences for our retrospective shock and grief. And for a significant moment for censorship shock – broadening moral change.

Dear *The Empire Strikes Back*,

A good friend, who has read the previous *Dear Movies* letters asked me last night whether I was writing to *Star Wars*. He seemed astonished (more than mildly) when I said that I hadn't intended to. He reminded me of all those *Star Wars* fans like him and seemed to indicate that I should acknowledge them, at least, with a letter.

So, I wondered which episode I would write to.

Actually, it took only a moment or so – no real competition. For me, you were the outright winner. Not that I haven't enjoyed the other episodes but, your impact in 1980 and the memories of your impact are still vividly with me.

In 1977, I was at a workshop in Gippsland and had to drive 100 km back to central Melbourne for the press preview of *Star Wars*. It was certainly different, being taken for the first time to that faraway galaxy and being introduced to that extraordinary world, storytelling and visualising that had an enormous effect on us, changing our perspectives on science fantasy, legends, and even some unexpected religious ruminations on The Force.

Perhaps I was a bit tired after the day's work and drive, or, perhaps, a little snooty in those days of reviewing because I seem to remember thinking that the dialogue in *Star Wars* had moments of the trite, a touch comic-strip (which in the 21st-century was to be the order of the day!). Maybe it was the dramatic heft of Alec Guinness being in it that made the night for me as well. He certainly gave a great gravitas to the Jedi and the role of Obi Wan Kenobi. Reports were he didn't quite understand the screenplay and of the plot but went along with it and humbly accepted a percentage of the box office (now that's financial acumen!).

Now that I'm reminiscing, I'm rather delighting in acknowledging the variety of characters as well as their exploits. Of course, Luke and Leia. And the laid-back humour of Harrison Ford as Han Solo (about to segue into the exploits of Indiana Jones). But I'm spending more memory time in bringing to life once again the affably lumbering Chewbacca, the mini R2 D2 and, of course, the prissy C3 PO. And not forgetting the image of Yoda and his Frank Oz wheezing didactic voice. Oh, and I just remembered Jabba the Hutt the rather oozy worm-alien – and was not sure in which film he appeared first so I googled and found the reference to Wookiepedia (truly). Actually, there is a long and serious Wikipedia entry – and the answer is that he appeared in *The Return of the Jedi* (with mentions in the first two released films).

I did want to express some disappointment in the least enjoyable of the *Star Wars* episodes – you may have heard this from others, *The Phantom Menace*. While it was welcome, and took audiences back to origins, it seemed a bit slight compared with the others and those which were to follow. Perhaps it is George Lucas, directing, he has shown himself to be a better storyteller and producer rather than director. And, despite Liam Neeson's earnest defence, I didn't warm at all to Jar Jar Binks. Shuddering just to remember him, postures, demeanour, and voice!

But, back to you.

It is forty years since you were first released and I haven't seen you since so I thought I'd better look up my review at the time. I think you will be pleased: 'By the end, one has been swept into the galactic adventures as before. Everybody (human and robot and Wookie) is back – characterisations somewhat stronger. The effects are quite spectacular: space, spaceships, asteroids and some excellent dinosaur-looking tanks; some of the rear projection work looks artificial. However, there is plenty of action, John Williams' score and the whetting of the appetite for more'. Of course, a special nod to John Williams now-so-familiar score.

But I have left to last the main theme that intrigued me. Darth Vader and the Dark Side, of course. While The Force has been a continual power and presence, a transcendent presence, a power for the good, in drama we are always intrigued by the evil Dark Side of The Force. We have some background that Darth Vader had been a Jedi Knight, inspired by The Force, but has gone over to, well, the words that have entered into our vocabulary and consciousness, the Dark Side. I still remember, and should watch the sequence again, where Luke confronts Darth Vader, the Dark Side leader trying to persuade Luke to join him, Luke looking into Darth Vader's face and seeing his own features and it is still chilling to hear, with James Earl Jones' sonorous voice, 'I am your father'. For me, one of the most surprising and even shocking sequences in cinema history.

And so, you are a spectacular as well as challenging exploration of the struggle between good and evil, the dark power of evil, even its persuasiveness, a revelation of conflict between father and son, horror at the evil that the Dark Side wrought throughout the Empire, and the challenge to hope in audiences who identified with Luke, the hero Skywalker, with Leia, his sister, and Han Solo and the heroics with his space-trekking associates.

So, just thinking of your long popularity, for those of us who tend towards the moralising have to offer you great thanks for presenting the perennial struggle between light and darkness, good and evil, so that it is has entered into the consciousness of young audiences worldwide for four decades. (And, I hope stays in the consciousness of the audiences as they grow older.) I will send this letter of to my friend hoping that I am in his good books again!

Dear *Kingdom of Heaven*,

I have just been writing to *The Empire Strikes Back*, crusades in a faraway galaxy long, long ago, the championing of the good of The Force against the pernicious Dark Side. Thinking of crusades, I thought I should come back down to earth, and the impact you made when I first saw you came to mind.

Cecil B. DeMille made *The Crusades* in 1935, glorifying the Christian enterprise for the freedom of the Holy Land 'the Third Crusade as it didn't happen' (according to the IMDb storyline). Twenty years later, there was a matinee entertainment along the same lines, *King Richard and the Crusaders*, Saladin getting top billing but played by Rex Harrison just before he became Professor Higgins! Those of us not as young as we used to be were brought up in a pro-crusades ethos, them and us! Those were certainly the days before inter-religious dialogue.

So, you brought a 21st century perspective to the events and the implications of those struggles between Christians and Muslims.

Ridley Scott, a prolific director of a range of genre films from *Alien* to *Thelma and Louise*, has made you a sweeping epic of knights and chivalry, of bloodthirsty battles, of wars between Christians and Muslims, of a dream and a short-lived attempt at multi-religious peace, the Kingdom of God, Kingdom of Heaven. You are set in the 1180s, between the second and the third crusades, the reign of Baldwin IV in the city whose name denotes peace, Jerusalem.

You remind us that the history of Christendom has been a history of war. God's name and God's will invoked to justify wars, even 'holy wars', many of which were sheer aggression, others of which were in defence of people's rights. 'God's will' has often been invoked, sometimes by both sides in a conflict, as motivation and justification for the battle. What passed for 'God's will' was often merely the whim of a leader.

The Crusades of the Middle Ages have been a sign of contradiction, some seeing them as an assertion of the rights of the church against 'infidels', sanctioned and blessed by popes and saints, others describing them as a bloodthirsty opportunity for land and power aggrandisement. You suggest that while Baldwin IV ruled in the Latin kingdom in Jerusalem, there was an attempt at mutual peace between Christians, Muslims and Jews, an attempt at creating the Kingdom of Heaven.

Scott and his screenwriter, William Monahan, with their western cultural backgrounds, have tried to be scrupulous in not being provocatively aggressive towards Islam. Since their perspective is that of the Crusaders, they opt for presenting the young Balian of Ibelin (Orlando Bloom) as the hero of the venture and adventure. He is written as a parallel to a 21st century Everyman, a seeker who has suffered the death of wife and child and a priest's damnation of his wife as a suicide, who has sinned in anger in killing the priest, who feels himself bereft of God's presence and joins his father's crusade to Jerusalem as a means for finding forgiveness and atonement. He believes that Jerusalem is a sacred place of redemption.

Balian, the Everyman, does not immediately re-discover God. During his crusading journey, he does become aware of his authentic humanity and tries to act with integrity, especially in the face of greedy and ambitious Christian barons who recklessly provoke war with the Saracens to bask in glory and possessions.

He is advised to make an oath to 'be without fear in the face of your enemies. Speak the truth, even if it leads to your death. Safeguard the helpless and do no wrong'. Right action according to conscience is to be his moral norm. You present Balian as a kind of contemporary secular saint for the audience. He is motivated by a spirituality rather than a religion (which is represented by a fanatical priest, a worldly and cowardly bishop as well as the wise Hospitaller).

It is always a matter of regret when official representatives of the church appear in such a bad light, but it would be foolish to deny that many such characters have lived in every era, wielding a destructive influence. The secular saint and the ecclesiastical villain can be seen as a constant and creative challenge to the believer.

Before you were released, you were the subject of both praise and critique, often sight unseen. Relationships between Islam and Christianity make for good copy as well as sensationalist headlines and opportunities for controversial marketing. Ridley Scott asked Islamic historian and cinema commentator, Hamid Dabashi, to be an advisor on your script and when you were completed. So you challenge Christian and western audiences to re-examine their traditions on war.

I am thinking of the biblical background. The Jewish scriptures are full of battles. The language of warriors is even used of God. However, as God interacted with the people, they learnt more of the ways of peace. By the time of Jesus, with the occupation of the Romans and the periodic uprisings, the language of the New Testament began to speak more of peace than of war. In fact, this is the message of Jesus, not only in the Sermon on the Mount where Jesus condemns the aggression and vindictiveness of an 'eye for an eye' theology of conflict and his advocating of a spirituality of loving one's enemies, but in a significant episode in Gethsemane. The disciple in Matthew's Gospel who draws his sword – it is Peter in John's account and makes us wonder what he was doing having a sword to draw – believes in physical violence to defend Jesus. This is the kind of motivation of the crusaders, at least of those who thought of the battle against 'the infidels' as a cause. And Jesus' response, his motivation, his strategy? 'Put your sword back into its sheath.' He goes on to what almost seems a pacifist stance: 'for all who take the sword will perish by the sword'.

You show us a range of warriors. Guy and Reynald think by the sword. They want power, land and possessions. They die by the sword. Baldwin, Godfrey of Ibelin and Tiberius have lived by the sword and have come to see how limited and destructive this is. It is the same in the range of Saracens shown. In a time when the worldview took battle and conquest for granted, Saladin and Balian, acknowledge that the safeguarding of the defenceless and of peace are more important than the battles.

Western audiences watching you see a range of stances on war parallel to those of the stances of the crusaders. The question to ask of Islam is what does the Quran say and teach about war? What are the popular conceptions of the jihad? What is the attitude towards Christians? Where are the meeting points on war and peace between the Gospels and the Quran? What is the 'spirituality' behind the character of Saladin, his safe conduct to the refugees from Jerusalem, his later dealings with Richard the Lionheart (who appears at the end) two decades later?

We realise that any dialogue between Muslim and Christian will have to go deeper than the long history of bitter battles and of persecutions. There is a peace founded on Jesus and his Gospel which must dialogue with a peace from the Quran. As Balian sits on the hill of Calvary, feeling bereft of God's presence, he looks down on the city whose name is peace in a land which might have become a multi-religious haven, the kingdom of Heaven.

Dear *The Rainmaker*,

John Grisham, of course.

I remember writing a letter to *Jack Reacher*, the Tom Cruise action movie, as standing in for Lee Child, all of whose thrillers I have read and enjoyed. So it seemed a good idea to write to a screen adaptation of a John Grisham novel. But, you may ask, why write to you?

There are several reasons. The first is that you were the first John Grisham novel I read. The 90s was the great decade for John Grisham movies. And I saw quite a number of them, and, because of this, I did not read those novels afterwards. I read the novel and then saw you, the movie. Another reason for writing to you is that I was very impressed by your screenplay, keeping so close to the novel's narrative and dramatising it so well. And I am reminded that Francis Ford Coppola not only directed you but wrote your screenplay.

And, there is what we might call a more proximate reason. At the end of the program, *Stars of the Silver Screen*, the episode on Roy Scheider, they showed a clip from your final court episode, Matt Damon as Rudy Baylor, interrogating him, Jon Voight as the leading defence counsel, contentedly smug before he is defeated. I was reminded of how much I liked you and that I'd thought of writing a letter to you. That evening, would you believe, glancing through the many lists of moves and movies available on Netflix, there you were. What else was there to do but click, 'Play ? And I wasn't sorry, you are both interesting and entertaining after twenty-three years since I saw you first.

And your cast. I had forgotten how many top actors you had, a credit to the casting director. And even some striking cameos from actors like Mickey Rourke, Virginia Madsen, Dean Stockwell, Roy Scheider. Jon Voight personified corporate legal, no scruples allowed. Danny DeVito was his hilarious self, somewhere between integrity and legal manipulation, but definitely closer to legal manipulation than integrity. Mary Kay Place was wonderful as the mother of the boy who died because the insurance company would not act on a claim for a bone marrow transfusion. And there is the young Clare Danes. And what a pleasure to see Teresa Wright in her last film, 55 years after her Oscar for *Mrs Miniver*. I was surprised, at the end, to find that Danny Glover, playing the astute judge, was uncredited. What a line-up.

And at the centre, was Matt Damon, 25 when he made the film, the eager young law graduate, no financial background, but wanting to make his mark. He was something like a young American Everyman, a young white American Everyman, eager and earnest, believing in the power of the law, its ability to change lives for the better, to change American society. You are a story of moral integrity.

Which makes you a much easier Grisham story to follow. While there are some complications, they do not really sidetrack us from Rudy Baylor's search and action for legal truth and applications of justice for suffering people.

Recently, during the covid-19 pandemic, in the context of the 2020 American presidential election campaigns, there was a significant article highlighting how our contemporary world, at least our Western world, had given up on integrity. At the same time, I saw an excellent documentary, *The Soul of America*, exploring the themes of journalist, former editor of *Newsweek*, Jon Meacham, released prior to the 2020 American election. In ninety minutes, Meacham covered a wide range of American history – the suffragist movement, the consequences of the depression, the 1940s internment of Japanese Americans, the 60s civil rights movement, the collapse of the Soviet Union, highlighting moments of integrity initiative. But he did give the statistic that American belief in government, 77% during the 1960s had now lowered to a contemporary 17%.

And so here is Rudy Baylor striving for integrity, initially sponsored by a luxury-driven shady lawyer (Mickey Rourke), advised by Danny DeVito as Deck Shifflet, generally on the right side but not troubled by any legal scruple. And Rudy, who had a harsh upbringing, discovers that he is dutifully a man of compassion, especially with the impoverished black family, bonding with the dying man, supporting his mother, dealing with the grief-stricken alcoholic father.

And so, his job becomes something of a quest, a mission, (and the expected cliché of David versus corporate Goliath in the insurance company whose policy is to initially refuse all claims). At times, he is inept, can foresee some of the pitfalls, doesn't have the experience to capitalise on situations. He is learning – and, at the end, seeing the company the subject of many class actions and declared bankrupt, he knows the key option for his life, integrity and understanding and, perhaps teaching, in law or to wake up and find himself the scoundrel lawyer that he has experienced in Jon Voight's smooth, superior, smug defence.

Yes, you do have a romance, the severely battered wife, a maniacal husband who batters her until she loves him. There are some melodramatic moments towards the end, occurring during the climax of the court case, but a simple solution and relief, and back to the courtroom.

There is always a great appeal in court room drama – the excitement of whether we side with the prosecutor or the defence, empathy for the plaintiffs, admiration (and frequent exasperation) with the cat and mouse tactics, the to-ing and fro-ing of legal argument, and upset at the bullying of so many witnesses. And, of course, that is what John Grisham excels at – which makes me wonder, I don't know if you can help, why have there been so few screen versions of his still-frequent novels since you were released in 1997.

Dear *The Last Full Measure*,

Discovering you was a surprise. I see that you had cinema release in the US in February 2020, just as Covid-19 hit. We didn't see you here – but then there you were on Netflix. I looked you up and found that you are a Vietnam story. And I also discovered that you had a very strong cast. If I had researched further, I would have found that your title is a quotation from Abraham Lincoln, from the Gettysburg Address, a reference to self-sacrifice in war, 'the last full measure of devotion'.

I'm very glad that I did find you.

With your Vietnam theme, it set me to thinking back about those war years. The war was significant for Australia, for a draft, our Prime Minister, Harold Holt, declaring 'all the Way with LBJ'. I do remember joining a picketing group outside the Canberra hotel where he was staying – but he avoided us and went in the back door. I also remember that boys that I taught in school in Canberra in 1966–1967, were serving in Vietnam in 1968. We watched the moratorium processions in capital cities. We saw the protests in the United States, Chicago 1968, shootings on campus grounds, My Lai, the Nixon involvement in the war, the bombing of Cambodia… All the way to the fall of Saigon in 1975.

Memories as well of refugees, Australia welcoming so many, their settling in high-rise buildings in Melbourne or, as we soon realised, isolated in the suburbs. We became very conscious of boat people and their dangerous voyages from Vietnam. But, and this seems strange, I don't have any memories of how the Vietnam veterans were treated when they came back home. There were plenty of stories from the United States, many of the movies, the hostility of the public and condemnation of the vets for several decades, although we saw *The Deer Hunter* and *Apocalypse Now*.

Watching you, I was moved because you are a film about men fighting in Vietnam, young men, out in the fields, ambushed, sudden deaths, injuries, helicopter rescue. But that is in your flashbacks because you are a story of 1999, an attempt to persuade the American government to award a Medal of Honour to a young man, Bill Pitsenbarger, who had given his last full measure of devotion in the field. A true story.

Your screenplay uses a powerful device to draw in your audiences. There has been a thirty-two year gap between action and this final request for the medal. There have been barriers, silences, cover-ups. And, once more, a weary application. A young man in a Pentagon office, Scott Huffman (Sebastian Stan), finds that he is assigned to this case. He is not particularly interested. There is to be a change of Secretary for his office. He is concerned about his own career and future, his wife and son. We are not particularly impressed by him.

But as he meets some of the veterans, meet the parents of the hero, is touched by his experiences in his encounters, we begin to identify with him much more, want to get to know the situation more, and, as each of the vets has nightmares, important flashbacks, we begin to appreciate who the young man was, his actions and decisions, his motivations, his willingness to give up his life for others. The whole narrative becomes something of a mission, of a quest.

Once again, your cast. You have quite a collection of veterans, solid actors for the 1999 sequences, Samuel L Jackson, withdrawn and fishing with his grandchildren; Ed Harris, looking rather emaciated, surviving; a shellshocked Peter Fonda, unable to sleep at night because of his memories and frightening dreams; William Hurt, part of the helicopter rescue squad, haunted by his efforts to persuade the young hero to come back to safety; John Savage, now retired to Vietnam, creating a sanctuary on the very grounds where the fatal operation took place.

And, most movingly, a dignified performance by Christopher Plummer as he was turning 90, the young man's father, battling terminal cancer, hoping for some kind of honour and vindication, Diane Ladd playing his wife.

Somebody remarked that they wanted more detail about the heroic young man. Rather, it seemed to me, better that we share the experience of Scott Huffman on his quest, gradually learning more and more, building up a final, more rounded, picture which made sense of the heroism.

But at the end, you bring us back to the bureaucracy, political ambitions, neglect by officers in bringing forward the truth, some snobbery concerning mere ordinary soldiers. Your screenplay is certainly no advocate of ambitious bureaucracy which lacks a sense of humanity.

And that's what you offer your audience – a significant re-visiting of American action in Vietnam, irrespective of whether one was in favour of the war or not, a story of men in war, limitations and strengths, responsibilities, suffering, injury and death, heroism in rescue, heroism in bonding with men under fire, willingness to die. The final award ceremony is significant but is highly emotional.

I notice that some comments about the award ceremony mentioned tears. You have that kind of gradual impact. I felt tears.

Dear *The Name of the Rose*,

Delving into history. That is something I like to do, something very important for me. So in the mid-1980s, like so many others, I ventured into reading Umberto Eco's novel on which you are based. Big mistake in a way. I couldn't make my way through it and gave up. I will keep that to the end, a touch of self-justification!

The novel made quite an impression in the mid-'80s - church history, an analysis of monasticism, philosophical reflection on theology and philosophy of the period, an examination of science, of language and linguistics. (Memories of 'A rose by any other name...' and Gertrude Stein's 'A rose is a rose is a rose.') Something of a challenge. You are meant to be a version of the novel, not its equivalent. In fact, your screenplay refers to a palimpsest of the novel. You captured much of the atmosphere of the novel, so I was told, as well as a great deal of its explorations.

I enjoy historical overviews – a sweep through 2000 years of church history in a two-hour theology lecture! And I also enjoy situating a historical episode in its context, its background and development. (At the moment I'm reading Sarah Dunant's novel *The Name of the Family*, the Borgia family, power intrigues, the status of the papacy, 1502, a worldly church, Machiavelli – which reminds me that I should look at the television series, *The Borgias*.)

And that is what I like about you, a situation in the early part of the 14th century, a century that really does not appeal to me at all, dubbed the decline of the High Middle Ages, the achievement of the 13th century in so many fields, and, just thinking of saints, Francis, Dominic, Thomas Aquinas and his theology come to mind, of Dante. But the 14th century! The Black Death plague at its centre. The collapse of central authority in the church, the seventy years of the papacy at Avignon instead of

Rome, the political squabbles, the disputes, combative claims, the Great Western Schism – something of a mess of a century.

You bring to life your setting of the vast Benedictine Abbey in northern Italy. It is an imposing presence, and you take us into its interiors, its life of prayer, liturgy and music, its life of study, the pharmacy, even into the kitchen and refectory. And the monks! In fact, it looks as though the producers went to Central Casting to find as many middle-aged and older men that look like Fellini-grotesques. There is Feodor Chaliapin as the sinister, Venerable Jorge. But monks are dying in mysterious locations. And Umberto Eco has created the master 14th century Franciscan friar-detective (with his evocative name in detection), William of Baskerville (also with echoes of the philosopher, William of Ockham and his famous Razor), visiting with his novice in tow, becoming more involved in the mysterious life and deaths in the monastery, one of Sean Connery's greatest performances.

And then the Inquisition! And who better to portray the Dominican inquisitor than F. Murray Abraham soon after his Oscar-winning portrayal of Salieri? While the inquisitor has the task of investigating the machinations within the monastery, trials and torture, he is also an official representative of the church and has to preside over a public disputation, Franciscan friars with their vow of poverty on the one side, church officials and visitors from Rome on the other stances that the church could own property. The dispute topic is: Did Jesus own his own clothes? On the one hand, this is theologically and spiritually interesting. On the other, it is a reminder that religious realities can be caught up in cerebral, over-articulated nitpicking arguments.

Speaking of nitpicking arguments, it is a mixture of intellectual delight and shock to discover the motivation of the murders, the danger in reading the *Poetics* of Aristotle, and the freeing power of catharsis in drama – and a theological connection to the power of laughter, laughter as enabling individuals and communities to be free, laughter as a danger in undermining authority. And the disputed question, did Jesus laugh? If he did, could his disciples? And if they did, would that give them too much freedom and be a danger to authority? Murder is done here in the name of this argument – authoritarian powers might not kill, but they can overbearingly destroy quality of life, and laughter.

Yes, you are an entertaining tale, an intriguing murder mystery and solution, history of the Inquisition, illustration of philosophy and theology and argumentation, an immersion into the decline of the Middle Ages.

And perhaps you're wondering why I did not persevere with Eco's novel. There is page after page after page of separate words, lists and lists and lists, catalogues. While this kind of writing might delight those who relish sense and senses, evocations, I find them wearisome and unreadable. I far prefer to be tantalised by mysteries and mysterious behaviour. So that is one of the main reasons, along with the delving into history, why I did enjoy seeing you.

Dear *Words on Bathroom Walls*,

Intriguing title when I first heard it without knowing anything about you. When I began my review, 'Recommended' was the first word that suggested itself.

Recommended, first of all, for younger audiences, high school age audiences, especially, who can identify with the central characters. They have limited experience of mental illnesses but may well have experienced them in fellow students. You offer an accessible opportunity for some understanding and some tolerance for their peers.

But, you can be recommended for older audiences, especially parents and grandparents, for teachers and those involved in youth education. They will have had much more experience of mental illness but this is an opportunity to see it dramatised within the space of your two hours.

One of your great advantages is that you have a very well-written screenplay by Nick Naveda from a novel by Julia Walton, intelligent and articulate, with a great deal of sadness, but also with some humour.

Young actor, Charlie Plummer, brings your central character, Adam, to vivid life. His situation is often dire. He is still at high school. His father has walked out. His mother, Beth (Molly Parker), is absolutely devoted to him, taking him to doctors and psychiatrists, eager to find the right medication and program, perhaps over-eager in her love and care. Many times, Adam finds this smothering, sometimes dominant and dominating. And your screenplay alerts audiences to prescriptions, medical programs, side effects, the dangers of not following the regime. Adam is antagonistic to Paul, his mother's boyfriend.

Often very affecting, you use visual devices to indicate Adam's schizophrenia and its effect on him. In various episodes, the images are blurred, sometimes a black pervasive smoke, distortions of people around him. For the voices that he hears, they are embodied in three characters: Joaquin, a fellow off-hand teenager, sex often on his mind, Rebecca, a sympathetic and encouraging young woman, and a Bodyguard, tough and fierce, with some supportingly fierce associates. They turn up (although not when he is on his medication regime). Adam also hears voices from open doors. And as for your title, it appears towards the end in a frightening hallucination of so many words of graffiti, denouncing his schizophrenia, on the toilet walls.

Adam is very frank about his schizophrenia. He sometimes explains himself, direct to camera, to a psychiatrist, talking to us. At school he has an episode and burns the arm of a fellow student, and is expelled. While he is not a Catholic, Adam is enrolled in a Catholic school, St Agatha's, the principal, Sister Catherine, strict but prepared to allow him to try.

I wasn't expecting it but there was a statue of the Sacred Heart, the chapel, a confessional. (And, Adam discovers some writing on the toilet wall, 'Jesus loves you, if you are not homosexual',) The Catholic theme is unexpectedly emphasised in the introduction of the character of Fr Patrick played by Andy Garcia. Adam wanders into the chapel, goes into the confessional, unfamiliar with what happens, but finding a very sympathetic priest who is able to listen, use common sense, is not judgmental, offers a range of Scripture texts (which Adam is not enthusiastic about), explains the nature of the confessional and how acknowledging one's limitations and faults can be liberating. (If only all the clergy had the genial characteristics of Fr Patrick!

Which brings us to Maya. She is Hispanic, the class valedictorian, has won many awards (and no hesitation in mentioning them), can look teachers and fellow-students in the eye. Self-assurance is her immediate impact. She has a system going where she writes essays for fellow students and, no holds barred in keeping them to their contracts and payment. She confronts Adam who has seen her in operation. She accosts him in the dining area, is clear and frank.

Adam is smitten, asks her to be his tutor. The relationship between Adam and Maya is sensitively portrayed, hardships, warmth, to love.

(I don't know if you are familiar with the Myers Briggs Type Indicator which derives from Carl Jung's Psychological Types but Maya leapt off the screen as an ENTJ – outgoing and decisive, strong-minded and intuitive. Usually more men identify with this Type – but think Margaret Thatcher and check out Meryl Streep as *The Iron Lady*.)

Maya drives an objective hard bargain in determining her tutoring fee. She makes good demands on Adam for his maths study and preparing a personalised essay for a possible scholarship. Adam has not revealed his schizophrenia to her but helps to win her over with a bit of down-to-earth experience. Adam wants to be a chef, has cooked for years and is expert at recipes, ingredients, and creating unexpected tastes. She is intrigued.

But there is another side of Maya. When Adam discovers that she comes from a poor family, her father out of work and she having to bring in some money, she loses that self-assurance, acts in uncertain ways, is caught in her emotions. She becomes more vulnerable. But she rescues herself, firm thinking back to her real self. While she is charmed by Adam inviting her to the Prom (which she abhors because it is a sign of the patriarchy), she does agree to go as long as everyone thinks she proposed the idea to Adam!

I was very taken with a further complication at home when Paul moves in with Beth and she becomes pregnant. Adam is determinedly hostile to Paul – although, ultimately, Adam has completely misjudged him, a quiet, discovering that he has been truly supportive. I was moved at an unobtrusively moving moment at the end when Adam is hearing voices and Paul quietly moves to close the door to stop the voices.

I had better sign off but let me say again, your performances make quite an impact. Your screenplay is able to communicate some of the aspects of schizophrenia, the episodes, the effect on the schizophrenic, misinterpretation and bullying by those who do not understand. I was right to have written 'Recommended'.

Dear *Nomadland*,

For an American audience, you offer an opportunity to look at the people of the United States, the part-time workers who wander the land in their vans and trailers, as well as a look in detail at the very land itself. And for non-American audiences, it is the same but it is also quite an eye-opener as you treks through the American nomadland in the various seasons of the year.

I was surprised to find that you had been directed by Chloe Zhao, who was born in Beijing. She has clearly absorbed the American experience, has written a screenplay, adapting it from a book by Jessica Bruder, has produced you, directed you and, making you very effective in your impact on the audience, edited you. You are a tribute to her intelligence and empathy as well as to her cinematic skills and storytelling.

And who could resist the presence of Frances McDormand (who took on the project and acted as one of your producers). Frances McDormand has such a distinctive screen presence and it is a pleasure to remember her two Oscars, *Fargo* and *Three Billboards Outside Ebbing, Missouri*. As she has grown older, not concerned in the least about how she appears, she has embodied women who have had hard experiences and survived. And that is certainly the case with her Fern, a widow who has seen her husband die of cancer, has lived in the town of Empire, Nevada, which in 2011 has had its gypsum factory fail, the town collapse and be deserted.

She has gone on the road – and we willingly go with her, in her trailer, which she has made comfortable in its interiors so that she can spend her life there. She has a home, she says, though not a house! She joins a vast community of nomads who have a calendar where they can find part-time work at the various seasons of the year. You show us Fern at work first in the huge packaging plant run by Amazon. Later she will work on the land, at an odd theme park with a huge dinosaur statue, in diners, cooking and washing up. But it is her choice, and she relishes this way of life, its being reinforced by a visit to her sister and family, to a short stay at the home of a friend whose family welcomes her.

By and large, your locations are in the American Midwest and south-west, scenes of the barren Dakotas, the derelict town in Nevada, nomad communities in Arizona – with an excursion to some mountains and to the coast. It is a distinctive American tour.

We are with Fern all the way. Your director focuses more than frequently on Frances McDormand's face, the range of expressions, the intensity, the peace, the actress almost giving a performance with her face alone.

But most significant, there are the nomads themselves. In a way, your screenplay is a series of vignettes, the range of people that Fern encounters at work, on the road, at garage sales, bartering, especially with her love of rocks, and a special friend, David Strathairn's David. But we are surely impressed by Fern's conversations with several of the nomads – in a sense they are showstoppers.

There is Linda May who works at the factory, getting older, chatty, making friends with Fern, making the sharing of the nomads so credible. There is Bob Wells who has started a community in Arizona where all the nomads can come, stay, share, tell their stories, be listened to and heard by Bob. There is young Derek who asks Fern for a cigarette, later encounters him on the road, who tells Fern his story, wanting to communicate with his girlfriend and Fern reciting Shakespeare, 'Can I compare thee to summer's day...' (Fern had been a part-time teacher).

But, most memorable, is Swanky, 75, diagnosed with terminal cancer, talking frankly and amiably with Fern, reminiscing about the travelling adventures of her past, of the vast cliff with swallow nests and the swarms of swallows, going on her way for more adventures until she dies, sending Fern a video of the cliff and the swallows. And Bob Wells leading a memorial celebration of

Swanky as her friends all put a stone on a cairn in her honour. And the discovery that Linda May, Bob Wells, Derek, Swanky are all nomads themselves and that this is their only screen appearance.

As I write to you, the Oscars have not been nominated. Surely you will be nominated in several categories – and, it would be an appropriate ending for 2020 and US turmoil for Nomadland to win Best Picture, an important and profound portrait.

P.S. April 2021 – congratulations on three Oscars, Picture, Director, Actress.

Dear *Hope Gap*,

Your title is a mixture of the gentle. I always like 'Hope'. But, 'Gap' sounds so harshly monosyllabic. So gutturally abrupt. How can the two combine? You are one of the few films that I knew nothing about as I produced my Film Critics' Association pass, received my ticket and signed the slip required to explain who I was, and went to one of my first screenings after the over three months of coronavirus lockdown in Melbourne – and cinemas closed for eight months. (A resurrected life, at least a resurrected reviewing life!)

I quickly discovered that Hope Gap is a place – near the Kentish Town of Seaford, close to Dover, the striking white cliffs. At English Channel level, when the tide goes out, there are rocks and rock pools. It is a walk where Jamie, and his parents, Edward and Grace, used to take him when he was young.

But Hope Gap is also symbolic. This is a story of a marriage, twenty-nine years, but ending – although it may have ended years earlier.

While I was watching you, I thought that if an audience wanted to find a film that showed a marriage in close-up, moments of extreme close-up, an increasing awareness of the gaps between husband and wife, then you had to be highly recommended. You are not an entertainment in the genial sense. Rather, you are compelling drama that is often quite disturbing.

It was a pleasure to discover your stars, Annette Bening and Bill Nighy, at their best. You also have the advantage of a strong screenplay by writer William Nicholson (whose range, I realised, extends from *Shadowlands*, the C.S. Lewis story, to *Gladiator*). Nicholson turns out also to be your director.

One of the difficulties in writing a story about a marriage breakup (and for the audience watching) is how much the writer takes sides with each protagonist. How much sympathy should there be for each? Can the screenplay be judgmental? And this is a particular difficulty while watching you. I am somewhat taken aback at having to say that Annette Bening's Grace comes across as very unsympathetic, rather obdurate, dissatisfied, forever asking questions, quibbling with words and, as her son Jamie (Josh O'Connor) requests her, to stop having a go at her husband. Grace is Catholic and goes to Mass, believes in the insoluble bond of marriage, cannot accept what is happening to her. And, she does focus, incessantly, on what is happening to her, dismissing what is happening to Edward even as she wants him to stay and then to come back.

Because Grace is so hard, difficult to identify with, it was a challenge for me, not so much for the heart, but for the head, to acknowledge intellectually how hurt she must be by the experience while finding it so hard to empathise.

On the other hand, I found it was not so difficult to be sympathetic to Edward, Bill Nighy playing a quiet man, touch of the scholar, trying to avoid conflict, but finally deciding to leave – and the revelation that he has been in a relationship with a student's mother, Angela, for a year.

Jamie, who has something of a lonely life of his own, is brought in as mediator, conveying messages, questions – fond of his father, but his mother then beginning to treat him in the same way as she treated her husband. Even more lack of sympathy for Grace.

So while this is life-threatening and life-changing to the protagonists, I realised that it is a hard (important) challenge for the audience to share these experiences.

There is a strong moment of dialogue, one that stays with me, when Grace confronts Angela, who says that she has seen them: there were three unhappy people – and now there is only one.

During your final credits, thinking that you would be the film I would suggest to anyone wanting a film about a marriage dissolving, collapsing you compelled me to observe, sympathise, avoid judgment, understand (as much as I could).

Dear *Mosul*,

I think I needed to see you. I think I needed to spend your one day in Mosul, war-ravaged, divided, to experience uncertainties, fears, sudden violence and death.

I knew the city of Mosul became well-known to the world at large with the American invasion of Iraq in 2003. And we've had years to ponder the instant devastation, the attack on Baghdad, the toppling of the statue of Saddam Hussein, the impact on the people of Iraq, the American presence, the realisation that mission was not accomplished... After 9/11, the next 21st-century experience to be regretted.

Then the Syrian civil war. For an outsider in the southern hemisphere, almost impossible to comprehend. There is simply an empathy in the mind. And then come the, for us, infrequent television news images, devastating bombings, the role of the Russians, Bashir al-Assad and his relentless government, the rebels, the destruction of Aleppo. Then, the world moved, for the moment, stunned by the photo of the forlorn dead body of that boy on the Turkish beach. Our keeping in touch with this war, the Syrian people's experience, the millions of refugees, the boats, The Greek Islands, barbed barriers, even into Eastern Europe, whether the country has any peace, is spasmodic.

And then, ISIS. We know that there was radicalisation in Australia, that there were departures, militant men, their wives and families, leaving to join the self-styled caliphate, easily severe interpretations of Islam, misogynistic, cleverly using social media for propaganda, grim and gruesome pictures of children, severed heads and executions, encouraging a network of brainwashing throughout the world for recruits. And the occupation of Mosul.

Just glancing over what I've written, it would seem that I've been carried away – but it was necessary, getting my mood in mind and emotions together as I reflect on my experience of watching you. Your action takes place over one day towards the end of the attempted caliphate. The city is divided, a free section, an occupied section, sometimes men, women and children trying to escape from the occupied section and being shot in the streets at the checkpoint by snipers. And a moving episode, two young boys carrying a coffin through the rubble streets.

The opening sequences tend, intentionally, to bewilder us. A young policeman and his partner are under siege from ISIS, many of their fellow-police dead. A special squad arrives, a SWAT team, led by an intense, staring, Major (Suhail Dubach is quite memorable, even haunting.). The young man and his associate have to prove themselves as not being ISIS. The Major has a very loyal squad.

The day's action highlights (and involves us, your audience) a number of episodes, a car exploding endangering the SWAT team, the decision to go back to the free part of the city, bribing an officer at the checkpoint so that there is no record of their moving backwards and forwards. There is a visit to another special squad, led by an Iranian, to get information, exchange cigarettes for weapons. There are skirmishes, snipers on roofs, scouting out of buildings for infiltration and attack, members being wounded, killed.

When the Major is out of action, the young policeman, wounded, but now roused, takes up the leadership, jingoistic, enthusiastic, violent. And you provide an emotional shock for us when we discover at the end what the mission for the SWAT team actually was – personal rescue, wife, son, family, a deeply humanitarian reminder of what ISIS seem to be against.

I am surprised to find that you were written and directed by an American, Matthew Michael Carnahan (whose credits include a number of action films), filmed in Arabic and some Iraqi dialects with an international cast, some of whom live in the United States.

The locations for filming were in Morocco – with a devastating reconstruction of the bombed and bombarded Mosul.

ISIS was defeated – but still lingers. Iraq continues on, efforts for rebuilding and stability go up and down. And the civil war in Syria? When will it end?

So you see how important it was to watch you for ninety minutes of immersion, and a challenge for empathy.

Dear *Mass Appeal*,

You are one of my favourite films about priests. You hit a chord in the mid-1980s. You were a play from the 1970s but you were released the year of the 20th anniversary of Vatican !!, 1985. Since I was a student in Rome during the four sessions of the Council, ordained there, and, in 1985, not long finished a stint in religious life formation from 1968-1983, you were more than topical for me. As I watched you, I was resonating with so much of what you were showing – but also looking on as an observer as you portrayed life in the American church and life in dioceses whereas my experience was all in the context of a religious order in Australia.

As I write to you, it is almost twenty-six years since you were released. And I am wondering whether in some ways you are stuck in your period. You mirror the difficulties of men in the seminary who came from a post-60s American/western culture. There were more vocations in those days – but diminishing considerably. Clergy were more numerous than now (much more numerous – and so much less older than they are now). Revelations about clerical sexual abuse were to come, the challenge of a ministry of empathy for survivors, disillusioned Catholics leaving a church burdened by much incomprehension about the scandal.

But be that as it may (or is), I wanted to share with you some of my memories and insights from seeing you.

You offer an initial ecclesiastical shock. A young jogger, Mark Dolson, asks questions during the dialogue sermon of parish priest, Fr Farley. In fact, he is a seminarian almost at the end of his training. The staff find him abrasive. When two seminarians are suddenly expelled for a friendship judged to be too close, he angrily attacks the seminary rector. When Fr Farley pleads for fairness for Mark, the rector asks him to take on the deacon in his parish to train him for a month and test his suitability for priesthood. Coached by Fr Farley for his first sermon, Mark falls back into his aggressive style and alienates the parishioners.

However, Fr Farley likes Mark's passion and tries to help him to a greater maturity. The young man has an effect on Fr Farley who is dependent on his parishioners liking him, who drinks too much and uses white lies to get out of doing what he doesn't want to do. They talk frankly to each other about their lives and their families.

So far, so important – and so different from seminary life and student acquiescence in the pre-Vatican II Church. Fr Farley gives Mark another chance at a sermon which is more heartfelt and is well received by the congregation.

I want to share with you some of my review at the time. Hard to realise that it is three and a half decades ago!! I wrote that you

> 'rang true echoing the changes in the American church after the Second Vatican Council. The film presents a picture of the Catholic Church in the United States in the 1970s and 1980s. It highlights the changes in the church since the Second Vatican Council, different styles of liturgy, seminary training, relationship with the laity. It also highlights the atmosphere of bureaucracy, the pressures (even to personal blackmail) for administration and decision making and in a greater openness in many clergy. The focus is on the challenge to a passionate young deacon for conforming with the established church. There is also the challenge to the priest who relies on his popularity with his parishioners to take a stance on principle.
>
> The movie's dialogue as well as the representation of a priest's life is authentic. The issues are serious, the writing is often humorous and employs Jack Lemmon's considerable skills and comic timing as Fr Farley. The film is entertaining on a surface level. It is also a film of meaning and depth below the surface with the clashes between the

more authoritarian, ecclesiastical clergy and the younger, sometimes brasher, seminarians and priests.'

A scene that comes to mind as I write to you is that where Jack Lemmon begins the Mass and stops, saying he can't go on. The experience with Mark has taken a toll in his assessment of his life and ministry, in his judgment on himself. He is a good man with painful memories of family clashes. He has fought the dislike of his congregation to win them over. He has, in mid-life, settled into a wisecracking, benign and, sometimes alcoholic, parish priest. Priests in those days were ageing and victims of burn-out (not always picked up by the hierarchy).

I realise that I have lived through various eras of the church, that I have been a priest for almost 56 years, that I have been associated with changes in formation and am pleased to tell you that we do have much better approaches to life and day-to-day reality than we did. Even though Pope Francis has been there for eight years and has boosted our confidence, who knows!

Dear *Some Like It Hot*,

I have been meaning to write to you for some time, one of my favourite films from way back. But I wanted to see you again if I could. And, it seemed and still seems a bit of a psychological challenge in retrospect, I missed pre-setting the recorder twice! And months passed and Fox Classics was not repeating you as often as usual. But since I'm now writing, you are programmed again (relief!), mission accomplished.

I see that many commentators consider that you are in the top ten of comedies of all time. Which made me wonder what were the ingredients which appealed to me long ago, have appealed to audiences for over six decades.

Probably the novelty of seeing Tony Curtis and Jack Lemmon as Josephine and Geraldine hiding out from gangster Spats Colombo and his south side Chicago Chapter after witnessing the St Valentine's Day Massacre – with an all-girls band. It wasn't quite the done thing in mainstream Hollywood movies in those days but the two actors carried it off perfectly. In fact, looking at you again, I'm in even more admiration for Jack Lemmon and his screen presence, perfectly absorbing the character of Geraldine, yet having his shock moments of reality as bass player, Jerry. Jack Lemmon so enters into the role that Geraldine becomes a credible character, full of witty response, repartee, wisecracks, delivered with perfect timing. And his dancing with veteran Joe E. Brown! And his emotional delirium in being engaged!

Which means that Tony Curtis can play the straight man, lots of response and repartee as well, the touch of the double entendre, the conman, especially in his wooing of Sugar. And, on looking at you again, I'm in more admiration for Marilyn Monroe. Perhaps we were a bit distracted in the past about her reputation, the range of films she was in, the sadness of her life, the breakdown of her marriages, and all the stories about her turning up late, the numerous takes, moodiness... But looking at you again, none of that can be discerned. She enters perfectly into the character of Sugar, the mixture of the ditzy and the shrewd, great self-confidence despite her thinking she wasn't, delivering her songs perfectly, caught up in the romance of trying to heal the impotent heir to the Shell fortune.

Lots of great comedy there.

However, I do have happy memories of the gangster framework of the story, the ingenuity of director Billy Wilder (and memories of Marilyn Monroe in *The Seven Year Itch*) and his witty co-writer I. A. L. Diamond. Masters of plot, masters of dialogue, intelligence and clever humour.

With George Raft as Spats, along with his two thug-mug bodyguards, and with Pat O'Brien as the sardonic detective, we are taken back, with them, into the gangster films of the 1930s. So a touch of homage, moments of nostalgia, car chases and machine guns in Chicago streets, the lining up of the victims in the garage on St Valentine's Day. But it reaches an ironic comic pitch at the banquet for Opera Lovers in Florida, the ironic speech of Little Bonaparte at the dinner, on the one hand this, on the other hand that... The hitman getting into the birthday cake, emerging and firing into the Chicago delegates, Josephine and Geraldine hiding at their feet under the table! And then the final pursuit...

Not sure whether I'm doing justice to you at all, but I wanted to let you know something of how I enjoyed you then and enjoy you now. And your ending – while Joe E. Brown as millionaire Osgood planning his wedding to Geraldine fobs off all Geraldine/Jerry's objections, there is his declaration, wig off, that he is a man. 'Nobody's perfect' has never sounded better. But it proves that some endings are perfect.

Dear *The Father*,

Bewilderment. That might be the key word for appreciating your powerful cinema experience. It is the bewilderment experienced by your central character, the elderly Anthony, retired, living in his flat, comfortable in its familiarity. But it is the bewilderment that your screenplay skilfully exercises on the audience, making us share in upsetting and mystifying experiences with Anthony.

Your screenplay (which I see won for Florian Zeller the Oscar for Best Adapted Screenplay) is based on your director's play, collaborating for the screen with the veteran playwright and screenwriter, Christopher Hampton (*Dangerous Liaisons, A Dangerous Method, Cheri*). As we. the audience, experience you, we come to realise how intricately clever your screenplay is, making us share Anthony's life – or his life as he sees it.

But it is brought to the screen by Anthony Hopkins in one of his greatest performances (and that is saying something). And he won a second Oscar. His character announces that he was born in December 1937 – and that is the date of Hopkins' own birth. Which means that he is acting a man his age, but playing a man who is not able to act his own age. Hopkins plays with great subtlety, often quiet, sometimes bombastic, seemingly sure of himself, then becoming – that keyword – bewildered.

For me, there was strong identification, remembering my own father in his final months, realising that visiting him after Mass in his room at Cluny, if he was sitting on the side of the bed, he had been wandering out and about and bewildered; but if he was lying in bed, waiting for breakfast, all was well. (Then another authentic reference with Anthony mentioning being in a circus and dancing, reminded me that, some years ago, a confrere suffering dementia confided to visitors that he had ridden an elephant in a circus.) I am sure many in your audience will be making the same kind of connections with their experience of aging relatives.

Your setting is a London that looks familiar out the window, streets, blocks of flats, the local park. Anthony is seen living in his quite comfortable flat. He is visited by his daughter, Anne (another quite different performance from Olivia Coleman, (*The Crown* as Queen Elizabeth, Oscar Winner for *The Favourite* as Queen Anne). We see her as middle-aged, divorced, looking after her father, bringing in food, cooking for him. However, she has met someone, Paul (Rufus Sewell) and is planning to move to Paris with him. Anthony objects, repeating his advice several times that they don't speak English in Paris.

And then we the audience become even more bewildered because suddenly Anne appears again, bringing chicken for his meal. But this time, as Anthony and we see her, she is played by Olivia Williams. So who is the real Anne? And further complications because Anthony suddenly finds a man sitting in his flat, reading the paper, unpleasantly telling him that he lives there and that Anthony doesn't, that he is Paul (this time Mark Gattis).

And there are even further complications, more bewilderment for Anthony and for us. He has been asserting his independence. He doesn't need a carer – and picks quarrels with all carers, dismissing them. However, Anne introduces him to a young carer, Laura (Imogen Poots), who momentarily gets on with him but then he taunts her and humiliates her. She does come back, trying to do her best.

And then the layout of the flat and its pictures change, and it is Anne's flat with mysterious corridors and doors. And then Anthony is in hospital, not happy. No bewilderment relief for him. But there is for us as we see the alternate Anne, alternate Paul, alternate Laura, as the hospital staff.

So what are you doing? What is your effect on us? We realise that we are being invited to share the experience of aging, of possibilities of dementia, of possibilities of Alzheimer's, experiences of senility and the consequent bewilderment. While there have been some powerful portrayals of aging and mental and emotional confusion on screen, you can be wholeheartedly recommended.

Dear *Path to War*, Dear *The Second Civil War*,

I'm giving myself an exception to the rule of one film per letter. Let me explain why I want to write to each of you and am writing to you together. In lockdown times, 2020-2021, there was a lot of television watching, and watching movies on streaming services. Foxtel began to show a series of television movies made during the 1990s and into the early 2000s. Most of them turned out to be very interesting indeed, especially the two of you.

Watching each of you, one very serious, one a very seriously comic satire, made me realise that I really enjoy films – preferably fictionalised – over documentary, that dramatise American politics. In the 40s and 50s, our movie awareness of the US was very much Cowboys and Indians – with a strong trend change in awareness of Native Americans with James Stewart in *Broken Arrow*, 1950, and Jeff Chandler a dignified Cochise. The Eisenhower era made very little cinema impact. However, with JFK...! There was the Catholic partisan support (and some later shocked moral disillusionment). Then the Berlin Wall, the Bay of Pigs, the Missiles of October, Kennedy's assassination. For me this was my first half of my 20s, living in Rome, thinking internationally (although, would you believe, with the opening of Vatican II so much concentration there that I actually missed the October 1962 missiles crisis!).

Then there was LBJ, Martin Luther King and Civil Rights, deeper immersion in the Vietnam war, 1968 and political assassinations, protests, the Nixon election. So many movies in the succeeding decades and so many exposés, *All the President's Men*... Vietnam films, portraits of presidents (thanks to Oliver Stone). Some were very topical. Others enabling us to look back in retrospect.

Which is what happened to me when watching, first, you, *Path to War*, John Frankenhiemer's last film, 2002. I had never heard of you – don't know why. But as I watched you, fascinated, intrigued, remembering the times (even going to protest against LBJ's visit to Australia in 1966 in Canberra), you offered the opportunity to evaluate and re-evaluate. Especially the Vietnam war looked at in retrospect. Which is what you were doing, dramatising the events almost forty years later. And here was I looking at your drama twenty years further on.

I had seen Bryan Cranston as well as Woody Harrelson portraying LBJ. But discovering Sir Michael Gambon as Johnson really bringing him to vivid life! Big, brash, prone to anger, yet skilled in politicking, working behind the scenes (a cameo sequence when Johnson cajoles racist Alabama governor, George Wallace, to moderate his stance quickly comes to mind). You open with the post election celebration, State of the Union address, 1965, elation. I was interested in what you presented about civil rights behind the scenes and Johnson's contact with Martin Luther King, his response to the Selma March. But there was ever the path to war.

You are very well and thoughtfully written, performances from a wide range of character actors, exemplary. Intriguing to watch and to think back about Clark Clifford, initially dovish then hawkish (embodied by Donald Sutherland) and, since we remember much more about him, of Alec Baldwin's career best performances as Robert McNamara, confidently hawkish, disturbed by protests, wanting more understanding. And the reminder, after all those cabinet meetings, listening to the rather warmongering generals (not concerned about civilian deaths' collateral), that with all the advice, the final decisions always rested with Johnson.

With all this in mind, I sat down to watch you, *The Second Civil War*, 1997 – but never having come across you, nor heard of you, having to check what this Civil War actually was. Once again, you have a vast expert cast of veteran performers. Your screenplay is both serious and often laugh-out-loud funny, by Canadian Martin Burke. And of all directors, Joe Dante –

whom we remember especially from his *Gremlins* films. But you are satirical targeting at key American issues. You were released in the Clinton era (and Beau Bridges secessionist Governor of Idaho reminds us of philandering leaders). There were issues of migration (Pakistani orphans after a nuclear disaster), preserving the American population from these inroads, the American dream.

You are set in the near future, three days when Idaho, full of angry militia types, confronted the rest of the United States well, not exactly, because more and more states, even the Chinese governor of Rhode Island resenting inroads of Chinese migration, began to support Idaho. Borders, military buildup on each side, past rival generals reminiscing about old grudges (and appearing on television as if they were dignified in negotiating). A dithering President, cabinet members, a public relations expert (who forbade the L word, lobbyist), advising the president to be a hawkish Teddy Roosevelt, statesman like FDR, aggressive like Truman, dignified like Eisenhower... And the deadline undermined by a climactic episode of *All My Sons* which the whole of the nation would be watching at the moment of the exploration of the timetable for peace.

But the focus is the media, CNN-like, frantic boss, wanting ratings, international and local reporters (and some funny shenanigans a touch reminiscent of *M*A*S*H*), but a dignified anchor-presence with James Earl Jones, political stances and voice-over.

You were relevant in 1997. BUT... We are watching you in 2021 and, of course, you've guessed it. We actually lived through most of your screenplay from the 2016 presidential campaign to Donald Trump's defeat in 2020. As we watch you, we realise how prescient you were, and, as we laughed with and at your comedy, wondered how the United States and the rest of us actually lived through the turmoil, the divisions, the sloganeering, the whims of the President, and, gasped in disbelief, with the 6 January 2021 invasion of the Capitol by the types which had been set up by you.

2021. Joe Biden is president. May peace be upon us all.

Dear *Shutter Island*,

I remember looking forward very keenly to seeing you on first release. I very much enjoyed the film versions of Denis Lehane's *Mystic River* and *Gone, Baby Gone*. He writes solidly intriguing novels. But, surprisingly, you are very different. And you are different from most of Martin Scorsese's films – and, a confession, I much prefer you to his (excellent) gangster films. So I took the opportunity recently to watch you again. And to look up my review and be cheered on finding that the elements I appreciate now I commented on back then…

I was wondering whether my review had mentioned the date of your action, 1954. That was a period of psychological experimentation in rather grim, what they call Victorian, asylums (to be seen in such films of the 1940s like *The Snake Pit* and *Dark Corner*). Gothic is another apt descriptor. You have a very sinister fortification building from the Civil War times, foreboding on the outside and dark and fearful in the corridors and cells inside. And you have the isolated lighthouse tower below the cliffs, waves smashing. And, come to think of it, in terms of 20th century psychology development, you are set only fifteen years after Sigmund Freud's death in 1939.

The other striking thing, of course, is the impact of the flashbacks to the concentration camp in Dachau and its liberation, the now-familiar grim picture of prison-garbed bodies, the emaciated survivors, the reaction of the guards, denial, surprise, dismay, summarily shot. You brought back memories that in 1966 I took the opportunity to visit the camp at Dachau, having to ask for directions and walk some distance from the railway station, a sombre experience and now realising it was merely twenty-one years after the end of the war and the liberation.

You certainly have a distinctive atmosphere which tantalises, invites but yet has a quality of repulsion. As I looked at you this time, I realised how carefully every shot has been framed, the atmospheric lighting and darkness, the intensity of close-ups, the wintry look of the exteriors, the frightening black of the interiors, and so much in a raging storm. And the range of the musical score, a melange of music from a range of composers, from pounding chords, cacophonous tones and classics like Mahler.

You begin like a police thriller, inviting is into an investigation, the ferry from Boston city out to the looming and ominous Shutter Island. And we were certainly interested to see how Leonardo DiCaprio is a US Marshal, in yet another Scorsese film. And Mark Ruffalo was an effective co-Marshal. On the island, Ben Kingsley seemed a perfectly rational psychologist, easily discussing therapy, critical of over prescription of drugs, of the violently intrusive procedures like lobotomy, treatment and therapy by punishment. On the other hand, there was something sinister with Max von Sydow and Nazi suggestions and undertones. And as the Marshalls proceeded on their investigation as to the disappearance of the mother who had murdered her children, there was a lot of talk about psychology, procedures, interviews with deluded patients, veiled warnings...

But your screenplay has a lot of continually intriguing elements, the identity of the woman who had disappeared, then her suddenly being found and explanations of her fantasy world with her children, imagining that everybody, everything was nice and orderly. But there were DiCaprio's flashbacks – his wife, death in a fire, suspicions of the man who started the fire and finding him on Shutter Island, the role of the police, and our realising that he was having his own delusions, his wife continually appearing, warning him. And then, his being out and about, searching the grounds, discovering the psychiatrist in taking refuge in the cave.

You have some rather overwhelming sequences, the dark encounter with the mysterious friend/or fire-lighter in the cell, the growing torment of the Marshall, making his desperately dangerous way to the tower.

You are certainly a film about mental conditions, mental illness, delusions, their consequences, separating the individual from reality. And while sharing the Marshall's bewilderment and recognising his denial, listening to the various doctors, their decisions about their treatment, the long time, the different methods, the personal doctor posing as the Marshall, you force us to reassess our attitudes towards mental illness. And the final forcing of the Marshall to face the reality of what he had done, the frightening re-enactment, stop us in our judgments.

And you finish with the tantalising question posed by Leonardo DiCaprio as to what is better – living a long life in the calm and happiness of the delusion or facing the ever-present harsh reality with its lifelong misery.

Dear *Remember*,

Over the years, I have seen many films about the Holocaust, been deeply shocked, moved, puzzled, dismayed at the bigoted depravity of human nature, compassion elicited for the millions who suffered in the camps, and the heritage for their children. I have written in the past to *Schindler's List*. I don't know why but watching you had a most powerful impact. I concluded in my review: 'a film that can be thoroughly recommended and, after the final ten minutes of the film, even more thoroughly recommended'.

I had been drawn to you because you were directed by the celebrated Canadian director, Atom Egoyan, who has been making powerful and striking films since the 1980s (and has won several ecumenical awards over the decades for *Family Viewing, The Sweet Hereafter, Adoration*). And I saw you during an Australian screening of a series of films about the Holocaust. But your setting is 2015, over 70 years later. As your title indicates, we have to remember – and explore the theme of memories, sadness, lies and deception, dementia and confusion, retribution.

Also, one of the reasons to see you is Christopher Plummer, at the age of 85, portraying a man nearly 90, Zev Guttman, a survivor of Auschwitz, where all of his family were killed. He is in a nursing home, suffering from confusion and moments of dementia, especially concerning his wife, always calling out to her, seeks her when he wakes. But she has died two weeks previously. In the nursing home, he has found a friend, Max (Martin Landau – 86 when he made you and gives a powerful performance) who has been tracking down Nazis, associated with Simon Wiesenthal and his Nazi-hunting, who helps Zev with the ritual celebrations in memory of his wife, and gives Zev a letter and a task to track down a commandant from Auschwitz who is responsible for the murder of families.

Christopher Plummer is in every scene, eliciting sympathy, eliciting concern, eliciting apprehension as he leaves the nursing home, takes a train with a prepaid ticket and an envelope of cash from Max, and pursues each of the names on the list to try to track down the officer from Auschwitz who has used the name Rudi Kurlander. In his quest, he finds several Rudi Kurlanders, two of whom are played strikingly by the German veteran actors Bruno Ganz and Jurgen Prochnow.

He travels across the United States with its extraordinary scenic beauty, going over the border into Canada, finally travelling by bus to Idaho, to Reno and to his final destination outside Tahoe. Meanwhile, his son and his wife are anxious about their father and his disappearance, eventually tracking him down at a dramatic moment.

We share the travel with Zev, every moment of the way. He elicits our compassion and concern. There are some difficulties as he journeys, people suspicious, questioning of memories, exposures of harsh truths. You make us want him to discover the true Rudi Kurlander, to confront him with his cruelty in Auschwitz, to make him see the horror of what he has done, the consequences on his victims, to admit, to confess, to accept responsibility, to repent, even to atone. And we do meet the true Rudi Kurlander.

You are a film to be seen, felt (more deeply than we ever expected) rather than described. You are particularly well written, tightly-written by Benjamin August, an atmospheric score by Mychael Danna, the excellent performances. And we, the audience, being absorbed as well as disturbed, even up till the shock of your final moment when your title finally comes up on screen. I'm not sure that you have been widely seen – but, again as I said in my review, you are thoroughly recommended.

Dear *Worth*,

I just heard a radio critic telling the host that watching you was his media highlight of the week. I was very impressed when I saw you. And you have stayed in my mind and, with the 20th anniversary of 9/11 last weekend, thinking more about you – and aspects of the disaster that I had never thought of.

Worth is a good word, a solid word. It takes us into the realm of values. In fact, your original title was *What Is Life Worth?* In fact, as we watch you and your exploration of characters, we are continually being asked 'What is a life worth?'. And how is this question to be answered? In monetary terms, a financial figure? Or beyond that?

The question was asked in the United States after 9/11 and you are receiving your release, at the Sundance Film Festival and, then, on Netflix, on this 20th anniversary of those planes crashing into the World Trade Centre and the Pentagon. At the time, the world was preoccupied with the immediate loss of life, the consequences, grief, amazement, continuing health problems, as well as the broader aspects of what became the war on terror and the invasion of Afghanistan (sadly and the hasty withdrawal ironically coming to a close on the 20th anniversary).

But there were financial questions asked – issues of insurance, the air companies' lobby, compensation by the American government, issues in Congress. With *Worth*, we are taken into this particular aspect of 9/11, a process from 2001 to 2003, the 9/11 Victim Compensation Fund, with prominent legal mediator, Kenneth Feinberg, accepting the role.

Soon into watching you, the pause button – because it seemed a good idea to go to Wikipedia and find out something about

Kenneth Feinberg, his background, his legal history, his role with the Compensation Fund, his principles. This exercise was enabling for continuing to watch you and appreciating what Feinberg hoped for, what he did, the challenges, his achievement (and, rather jaw-dropping, the final credits listing of situations in American history in the last twenty years, disasters, compensations, Catholic Church abuse cases... that he and his colleague, Camille Biros, have been asked to mediate).

Michael Keaton, a wonderful comedian in the past, has been taking on more and more serious roles, men of integrity, especially former Attorney General, John Mitchell, in *The Trial of the Chicago 7*. Amy Ryan gives solid support as Camille. And a range of character actors takes on supporting roles convincingly. But, as you progress, there are numerous interview sequences, survivors telling their stories, some angry, some still grieving, some bewildered. These are so convincing – and, one hopes, that the short segments serve as audition material for future roles by these character actors.

The other chief character is Charles Wolf, played by Stanley Tucci, an actual character, who lost his wife in the World Trade Centre collapse. Wolf was highly critical of Feinberg's model for the fund, starting a counter-movement 'Fix the Fund', offering advice, offering a different perspective on contact with survivors and their relatives, meeting with Feinberg and his associates, influencing Feinberg and his approach, ultimately with the declaration, 'The Fund is Fixed', finally ensuring that the Victim Compensation Fund requirements for registration were filled in time for the project to go into action.

For those of a Jungian frame of mind, you offer a powerfully dramatised presentation of objective structures for funding compensation relying on the letter of the law, accuracy and precision, setting limits, eschewing exceptions. Charles Wolf's approach was highly personal, much more subjective in respect of and respect for those who grieved and suffered, listening to stories, realising that categories could be constricting and that there were interpretations to be made. Two particular stories come to the fore to illustrate this – a fireman killed and his loyal wife's discovery that he had another family who are in financial need, a gay man who lost his partner (whose parents deny his sexual orientation).

It is rather saddening to read some bloggers dismissing you as boring. Others declared that they were engrossed, moved, sharing an experience of realising what a life is worth. Yes.

Dear *Hail, Caesar*,

Self-indulgence. A lot of cinema nostalgia. Those are the answers. What is the question? It's simply, 'Why am I writing a letter to you?'.

The Coen Brothers have had over thirty years of success in making films, great critical success, audience fans, Oscars and awards from festivals including Cannes. Perhaps, over all these years, they have had a special secret Bucket List of all the movie genres they would like to work in. And their output has been quite varied. With you, they seem to be putting into practice all those wishes. And successfully, both as homage as well as spoof.

Your title. Hollywood, 1951, a Roman epic called *Hail, Caesar*. This offers an opportunity to have ranks and ranks of marching Roman legions, slaves in captivity, and a star for the leader of the legions, Autolychus, George Clooney – adept at speaking some hammy lines, hammy performance as well as getting himself abducted by an alleged study group, naming themselves The Future, actually a Communist cell, giving Clooney lectures on politics and economics, on dialectic, with, of all people, the thinker, Herbert Marcuse (John Bluthal), present in the group for discussions. More than shades of the anti-Communist feeling of the time.

In fact, your focus is the manager of Capital Studios, Eddie Mannix, played very seriously with touches of irony by Josh Brolin. He is a fixer, on the phone to New York, getting reports from all the film locations, from the directors in the studios, handling temperaments, PR, arranged marriages, stars going into rehabilitation for drying out, dealing with the gossip columnists (in this case, two terrible twins both played very effectively and tartly by Tilda Swinton).

Recently, I was invited to take part in a radio conversation about cinema, some special emphasis on Coen Bros films. The other contributor was Jewish and wanted to talk about the Coen Brothers' very Jewish film, *A Serious Man*. Then it occurred to me to call you the Coen Brothers' Catholic film. And you are.

Your opening is very surprising for the Coen Brothers, a close-up of a crucifix, extreme close-up of Jesus on the cross, followed by an Eddie Mannix confessional sequence (later to be repeated more seriously – the priest in the confessional exasperated at his turning up so frequently to confess deceiving his wife about his chain-smoking). Eddie is a Catholic, proper, seen with his rosary, getting advice from the priest about a Lockhead job opportunity who reminds Eddie of the inner voice, the voice of God, and doing the right thing and for Eddie and his decision to stay with the studio.

He is also ecumenical for *Hail, Caesar*, because of the sequences with Jesus, the subtitle of *Hail, Caesar, a Tale of the Christ* (straight out of *Ben Hur*). He holds an interfaith consultation, the Orthodox presence and his worry about jumping from one speeding chariot to another! The Protestant representative talks with common sense. There is a Rabbi with sardonic comments on forbidding the image of God, but not of Jesus who was not God. The theological discussion with the priest raises aspects of the person of Jesus and theology, humanity and divinity, yes and no... But thinking the screenplay was respectful!

In fact, Jesus comes out very well, your reprisal of the Nazareth and cup of water sequence from *Ben Hur* as well as a final crucifixion scene with Autolychus coming to the cross and making a long speech (more heartfelt after his abduction and reprimands from Eddie), which could have fitted into any Crucifixion story – although tension is broken right at the end when Clooney forgets his keyword, 'faith', and the crew listening, rapt, then laughing. (You also have memories of *The Robe* and a small homage to *The Life of Brian* in Roman (mis)pronunciations.)

Before I finish this letter, let me enjoy some self-indulgence, remembering what it was like going to the pictures in the first half of the 1950s, the kinds of pictures that we enjoyed and took for granted. You have Alden Ehrenreich standing out as a cowboy in a B-budget Western where he can do somersaults on his horse, get caught on a tree branch and shoot his enemies and get back on his horse. He is an expert at the lasso, even with a string of spaghetti, and is seen singing in a romantic western scene. He is very funny when he is transferred, orders of New York, to go into a drawing-room drama where his cowboy gait and his terrible accent need the exasperated but charming attention of the director, played by Ralph Fiennes.

(We also have an excursion to the editing room for a cameo by Mrs Coen, Frances McDormand, smoking heavily and then her scarf getting caught in the projector and her almost choking!)

There is a musical with a reminder of *On the Town* and *South Pacific*, sailors ensemble dance led by the singing and dancing Channing Tatum – his character is revealed to have a much more complex side, to do with Clooney's abduction, a submarine and the Soviet Union. There is Scarlett Johansson doing an Esther Williams in a swimming sequence – exuding innocence until she opens her tough mouth and contract arguments and keeping professional secrets. Many, many things to enjoy and a solemnly British narration by Michael Gambon.

To my dismay, a good friend told me he didn't like you at all. And, scrolling through IMDb blog comments, I was even further dismayed at the horde of (philistine?) dislikes. If I can cheer you in any way, I am glad that you are one of my Dear Movies.

Dear *Riders of Justice*,

You took me completely by surprise. I was looking forward to seeing Mads Mikkelson, as always. But it took me a few moments, looking at the soldier with shaved head and full grey beard, and it was himself. I started my review, '*Riders of Justice* is quite an experience. No, that is something of an understatement. In its way, it is quite exhilarating'.

Your credits say that the screenplay, by the director, Anders Thomas Jensen and his associate, Nikolaj Arcel, is attributed to 'After an idea of...'. It would have been most interesting to be a fly on the wall as the two kept on getting more and more ideas, tossing them, tangling them, seeing how far they could go. In fact, if there were to be an award for screenplay which was completely unpredictable from moment to moment, sequence to sequence, *Riders of Justice* would be a top contender.

It might be possible to write your synopsis, though that would be an 'untangling' challenge, but very difficult to communicate (and the same goes for a reviewer) the changes of mood, the eccentricities of the characters, the funny repartee, the eruptions of violence. It probably should be mentioned that one of your main characters has continual Tourette's outbursts, no holds barred, and his syndrome seems to be infectious for most of the other characters. They do look graphic up there in the subtitles rather than simply hearing them. And, there are some shootouts and shoot ups (with the continual challenge as to whose side are we on).

Your introduction to the characters is arresting, Mathilde, a young girl, wanting a blue bicycle for Christmas from her Orthodox clerical grandfather; her military father phoning to say he cannot return for three months; a boardroom meeting with two fascinatingly eccentric characters who are putting a proposal, an almost incomprehensible spiel, about using statistics for predictions – they are fired! But, mother and daughter and one of the eccentrics find themselves together on a train, an explosion, the mother killed. And the statistician noting the suspicious behaviour of a passenger, going to the police with this information, but not really believed. Actually, looking at the characters and listening to them, who would believe them? But, each of them in his own way is quite obsessive, caught up in theory, but also one of them being an absolute expert in hacking, and their having another friend whose life is absorbed by hacking, collating information, extraordinary resources – so that the three are able to identify the suspicious man on the train.

And, the wonderful revelation of the Egyptian man and their identifying him. Wrong – and the hilarious scene of his explaining his horror of the sandwich and drink he deposited in the trains' garbage bin. So, he went and got McDonalds. (You are full of this kind of entertaining, ironical vignettes.)

In the meantime, the military man comes home, tries to relate to his daughter, failing. She is also interested in the chain of events, the unpredictable happenings that led to the tragedy, a series of post-its on her bedroom wall. Later, you have some nice, peaceable moments, the statistician and Mathilde having a long conversation about the nature of events, happenings, coincidences, the various strands of life that lead to an event in the human mind unable to comprehend it all.

If this sounds intriguing to a potential audience, then you and the developments in your screenplay are much, much more intriguing. The three experts, looking and acting like a variation on the Three Stooges, team up with the military man, identifying the criminals, a tattooed man on the train with his lawyer, about to testify against the bikie gang, Riders of Justice. It all seems logical, given the technology, and the three obsessive experts move into the military man's barn, a huge headquarters to probe the case. Actually, I very much enjoyed how the plan keeps going skew-whiff, including deaths, shooting, the rescuing of a male escort from Ukraine who ends up doing the equivalent of au pair work with the daughter. Also in the act is her boyfriend, a smart cook whose recipes appear online – which ultimately has dangerous consequences.

I should note how much is made of psychology (quite a lot of jargon), sessions of grief, therapy, counselling, one of the eccentrics having to take over as a therapist (with the mention that in his own life he had had several thousand hours of therapy so knew what he was doing) – and some of the sessions both effective and funny.

While Mads gives another, often manic, performance, the three friends are terrific, each in his own way, but some admiration for Nicolas Bro, often a substantial presence in Danish films. With his OCD, Tourette's, skill in assembling rifles and wanting to be a gung-ho shooter (and happily jokey about how large he has become), he stands out. Oh, and not forgetting Andrea Reich Gadeborg, quite young, but holding her own with the rest of the cast, bringing something of a gentle touch and emotion.

Not sure whether this letter is doing you justice for anyone reading it, but you are an experience of deadly serious episodes combined with ironic farce, shudder one moment, smile and laugh the next. And, the final shootout could be in serious competition with *The Wild Bunch*. But, at the end, some smiles, but it is Christmas, each receiving a gift, a French horn rendering of *The Drummer Boy*, Mathilde on her bike in the snow, and some tears forming in the eyes of the audience.

Dear *Free Guy*,

I have never played a computer game in my life (though some games of Solitaire on the computer!). But, over the decades, I've seen quite a number of films about games, gamers, men and women glued to their screens, firing off shots, vanquishing...

So my expectations of watching and enjoying you, were not particularly high, but your advertisements were around for a very long time in our first Melbourne lockdown, Ryan Reynolds bemused face looking out at us, so some hopes for comedy. You would be just about to be released and we went into another three months lockdown. You were on my list to catch up with when restrictions were lifted when, suddenly, you were programmed on a Saturday night on Foxtel. I settled back, a smile on my face, and apart from thinking about the equivalent of Truman in Peter Weir's *The Truman Show*, (Truman unwittingly and cheerfully locked in a popular television show all his life), ready to enter the gaming world. And, there was Guy, twenty years after Truman, cheerful and unwittingly ('don't have a good day – have a great day!'), Going through his daily routines, cereal for breakfast, bank robbery in the afternoon, all these strange bespectacled avatars, a nice guy.

Being of a generation where a tutorial on how computer games work is essential, the creativity of the minds behind them, the imaginations, of what the effect is on the gamers – and an explanation of the gamers and the visualising of their avatars on screen – I was not so caught up in the technology but the emerging themes. Free Guy! Free City! Freedom? (After the final credits, I glanced at the IMDb and began to scan the many bloggers to find how many mentioned themes of the quality of human life, human choice, freedoms – and found two (all the rest gleefully commenting on what a fun movie you are) and one of the these commenters thought your screenplay was too preachy!

I suppose a word is in order to praise the technological ingenuity of bringing a computer game world to the screen, the characters, dialogue, behaviour, adventures and dangers, the inventiveness of the CGI. But, I am more prone to notice and investigate themes.

So, Guy turns out to be a technological breakthrough, a games' character with artificial intelligence, on the edge of moving to decision-making. Guy puts on avatar sunglasses and sees aspects of the game he never dreamt of. And he sees Molotovgirl and is attracted. She turns out to be part of Millie, one of the creators of the game, working with her friend, Keys.

So, we have something of an online romance, poor old Keys (young Keys, pining in the background for Millie, but committed to developing Guy and letting him, as Jesus had said, have life and have it to the full). Obviously philosophical issues and, by implication, religious. People always complain that God should intervene in times of suffering. However, here is Free City, the inhabitants all happy, no matter what, living a kind of happy fatefulness. And then the discovery of freedom, choice, free will – and most of them initially reluctant. There are moments of great joy as we follow Guy and Millie in discoveries from bubblegum ice cream to the implications of Guy's first kiss. I especially enjoyed the appearance of Dude, Guy's inner self, inner alter ego, big, tall, musclebound, and the moment when the laser sword appears in Guy's hand, the *Star Wars*' theme commences and, intimations of transcendence, The Force is with him.

But, if the games creators are the equivalent of God, there is also a devil-figure. He is CEO Antwan and I've always enjoyed Taika Waititi's New Ziland accent. He is jealous of the creations as Lucifer had been. Profit is his goal. Any thwarting leads to destruction.

Antwan is too clever for himself, greed his downfall and self-deception. Millie and Keys realise that the games characters were computer incarnations of themselves and find love, Guy able to tell Molotovgirl that, despite her love, she could not live in his world. And he and Dude, along with Buddy his security guard close friend and the various characters in Free City, now have lives of their own.

And one has the perennial hope that life and behaviour for Guy and his friends in Free City will not fall into the traps and temptations to people that are part of real life.

Yesterday, before I watched you on Foxtel, it never occurred to me that I would be writing you a letter like this, nor so soon. I enjoyed watching you and thinking about you afterwards very much. And I did like the message, better to watch the computer games characters than to be shooting at them.

Dear *Blue Bayou*,

Even as I was watching you, I felt I was being put through the wringer. Naturally, I was hoping that everything would be resolved, for a happy ending; after all, you are an American film and that's what we might expect. But, no, with the final image and all through the credits, I felt I was still being squeezed through the wringer.

Kept wondering why I was so involved. The central character, Antonio Leblanc, Korean orphan, migrating to the US at the age of three in the 1980s, adopted, abused, discarded, stealing felonies, was nevertheless a most engaging character, a credit to Justin Tom (who has written your screenplay, directs and acts), American born but with his own Korean heritage, creating such a likeable man, joyful father delightfully playing with his stepdaughter, a caring husband to his pregnant American wife, all my sympathy despite his limitations. Of course, it was the migrant issues, especially the dramatic highlighting of deportations that gripped me.

Because this means that I was watching with Australian eyes, memories of the post-World War II migrations, the 'New Australians', acceptance of the British, the Poms, but wariness of the Italians and Greeks, dagos, Poles and migrants from other countries of Europe. It means memories of the experience of the acceptance of refugees from Vietnam in the 1970s and 1980s, much more acceptance here. And, then, twenty years of boat people, of turn backs, of engagement against people smugglers, harsher and harsher legislation, refusal of entry to boat people, calling them illegal even though they had rights to refugee status, Muslims, Middle East, isolation on Nauru, on PNG's Manus Island, years and years of harshness, stagnation, futures denied.

And, more to the point, the years of the experience of the Sri Lankan family in Queensland's Biloela, accepted by the community and welcomed, yet their being taken, isolated on Christmas Island, kept in custody, years and years of legal wrangles about the refugee status, imminent threats of deportation, but the nationality of their children, the possibilities of compassionate intervention by politicians – but none forthcoming.

You see, I was ready to be put through the wringer even before I went into the cinema.

I was surprised to discover the number of Korean and Asian children – apart from Vietnamese – who had been adopted. I wasn't able to follow all the details of legislation about adoptions, rights, citizenship, times and dates on which residency and deportation depended. All very complicated, bureaucratic.

But, here was the story of Antonio, sympathetic as I mentioned, supported by his pregnant wife and loved by her little daughter. But, prejudice and racism forever hovering. His mother-in-law unwilling to speak to him, ready to snatch her granddaughter away from him. His wife's former husband, policeman and angry, and the aggressive hostility, even to getting his buddies to bash Antonio, preventing him from getting to the court in time for his hearing. And there was the back story of his adopting parents, his unwillingness to make contact with his mother, eventually going to see her, his and our being puzzled at her behaviour towards him during his pleading visit.

And your screenplay does not make Antonio out to be a saint. Not only has he stolen in the past, his felonies and race preventing him in the opening interview from being given a job as a mechanic, but to get the money for the lawyer for his case, he and his friends steal more motorbikes. We realise that according to the letter of the law, authorities will not easily grant him citizenship. Your screenplay does not offer simplistically sympathetic solutions.

And, then there was Antonio's encounter with the Vietnamese refugee, Parker, her kindness at the hospital, meeting him in the street when advertising his tattoo studio, desperately in need of funds to pay for a lawyer to fight his deportation case, inviting him to her home for a Vietnamese gathering meal, her genial father,

Antonio asking whether he regretted dividing his family on the boats escaping Vietnam and his replying 'never', Parker's visit again for another tattoo and Antonio's harsh dismissal, her terminal cancer, their talking, the sadness of her death.

If only those against migration or those who say they are for migration but are rigid in their interpretation of laws, rules and regulations, could sit down quietly and watch your story, get to know your characters from the inside, and be moved.

P.S. It seemed I would never be writing this news. A new government in Australia, May 2022, the Biloela family released, allowed to return to Biloela, and their getting permanent visas. The seemingly impossible can happen.

Dear *One Second*,

I have been wanting to write a letter to one of Zhang Yimou's films for quite some time. At first, I thought of writing to *Raise the Red Lantern*, a wonderful entry into Chinese history, memorable for its colourful beauty. But I did not get around to it. And now I have just seen you, *One Second*. You reminded me that Zhang Yimou began directing films at age 37 in 1988 with *Red Sorghum*, making an impact with his drama, history, photographic beauty. This continued during the 1990s, with *Qui Ju*, *To Live*. But after the impact of *Crouching Tiger, Hidden Dragon*, which he admired, he made a great number of spectacular and colourful historical martial arts epics. I haven't forgotten that he was the chief director of the opening and closing ceremonies of the Beijing Olympics in 2008. During the 2010s, he has tackled a variety of themes and styles. The martial arts stories were quite engaging and enjoyable but he was not the only one making this kind of action film.

However, I fondly remember that in 1999-2000, he made two quietly domestic but very moving smaller films, *Not One Less* and *The Road Home*. For me, they were journeys into China, quieter and emotional journeys, meeting the people, familiar dilemmas and crises. You are very much in this vein and all the more welcome for it.

I almost saw you in Berlin in 2019 but you were withdrawn four days before screening, allegedly post-production problems, which most understood as some form of censorship and disagreement with your contents and/or its impact. It seems you were released in China in 2020. And, arriving here in Melbourne at the end of 2021.

I was very interested in your setting, 1975, the impact of the Cultural Revolution. And you are a story of cinema, travelling movie reels to remote rural towns, newsreels and propaganda films like the 1964 *Heroic Sons and Daughters*. I was pleased to see the sections of this film that you included, the audience rapt, having seen the films before, but singing along with the patriotic songs. Zhang Yimou has spoken of the 'collective experience' of these decades (noting that present generations are moving away to more individual experiences).

In many ways, your plot is small. You show us first a ragged man walking through the sand dunes (one commentator wryly noting that this is the most desert and sand dunes we see this side of the Rockies!). The individual is so small against the dunes. Who is he? It takes some time for us to find out as he wanders the desert, arriving in the town, too late to see the movie, encountering an orphan girl who steals a reel, pursuing her, recovering the reel and then losing it. So, not only who is he, but what is so important about the reel?

We have some sympathy for the man wandering the desert, clashing with the girl, recovering and losing the reel, getting lifts in trucks, eager to drink from the local tap, hungrily devouring noodles, and people regarding him as suspicious.

So, here we are, in a remote town, the people gathering, eager to watch the film – but a long episode, where a reel has fallen off the back of the cart and lies tangled in in the dust in the middle of the road. The stranger is desperate. The proud local projectionist takes charge and a huge cleaning, communal effort, follows.

And then we discover what the *One Second* is, a glimpse of film that the stranger eagerly wants to see, desperately wants to see. And we learn who he is, what his experience has been, what the sequence contains – pathos for him, pathos for us, the audience.

And there is more pathos when we learn who the orphan is, her studious little brother, the custom of making lampshades from film strips and the reason for her stealing the reel. Some bonding between the stranger and the orphan, after some fights, physical, some desperation on his part, some hurt for her brother on hers.

And then you seem to end sadly out there in the dunes. But, in fact, you have an epilogue, two years later, the Cultural Revolution over, prisoners freed, children better clothed and educated, and the stranger and the orphan meeting again, returning to the dunes, memories of sadness but, could we hope, a better future?

Thank you for helping me to achieve an ambition: to write a letter to a film by Zhang Yimou.

Dear *West Side Story* and Dear *West Side Story*,

Tonight, tonight. Tonight I went to the preview of you, 2021, Steven Spielberg's version, initially apprehensive with happy memories of 1961, then appreciating the experience, reminded of the past enjoyment, relishing the differences in developments. A happy night out.

And then my mind went back to 1962, Rome, sitting in the front row of a religious theatrette, looking right up at the big screen, the camera looking right down, overhead, on New York City and the streets. And, except for the songs, it was all dubbed in Italian. Russ Tamblyn as a Jet member had a deep Italian voice which didn't gel with him bursting into song with a rather more high-pitched crackly tone singing Officer Krupke. But, when I saw you again in later years, I re-lived that experience.

And now sixty years later, Steven Spielberg acknowledging that it was the key musical of his growing up, directs his first musical film. But, so many critics and audiences, wary of a remake, have praised you. For those who treasure the 1961 you, they will be happily reminded throughout the 2021 version of why they enjoyed their past experience so much.

But again, sixty years later, with the developments in technology, effects, cameras, editing, you are a very much a 21st-century version. Arthur Laurent's original book has been adapted by Pulitzer-prize-winning, Tony Kushner. You take us immediately taken into the rubble of New York, demolition of neighbourhoods around 68th Street (and an image of the about to be built Lincoln Centre). And, in the open spaces where homes once stood, the Jets and the Sharks begin immediately to rumble. And, we are reminded of the gangs' music and rhythms, the confrontations of Americans and Puerto Ricans, vicious, insulting, violent. And, with the rhythms starting, the beat, fingers snapping, we begin to anticipate all the rest of the familiar music, the songs.

One of the strengths of your version is that Tony, now played by Ansel Elgort, who actually sings his songs, is given a much stronger and credible background than earlier, the fact that he established the Jets with Riff, that he was very violent himself, has spent a year in Sing Sing, but has looked into himself and wants to change. Riff and the others certainly don't want to change. They are full of resentment. They want to fight, they want to rumble. And there are the police, the chief, as well as the officer immortalised in the song, Officer Krupke.

And Rachel Zigler, with her Hispanic background, is more realistic than Natalie Wood was. However, Arianna De Bose, already winning awards for Best Supporting Actress, is a powerhouse as Anita, singing, dancing, dramatic, and the whirlwind exuberance of the song and dance, in America (now with crowds in the streets). As we watch her, we are reminded of Rita Moreno and her vitality in that role.

And here is Rita Moreno, turning 90 (December 2021), playing a significant factor, Valentina, widow of the drug store owner, who gives shelter to Tony, who supports Anita and Maria, who defies the Jets. She has several powerful scenes and it is she who sings *Somewhere*...

The familiar scenes are there, the fights, the police interventions, the attempted harmony with the dance where Tony and Maria see each other, a Romeo and Juliet neighbourhood balcony sequence, some religious aura as they make vows to each other, the inevitable rumble, knives drawn, deaths. And a fine ending with Jets and Sharks, Maria following, carrying Tony's body, a cortege, very Shakespearean. And, as Shakespeare once told the story, wrong messages, deaths and tragedy, star-crossed lovers.

There's certainly a place somewhere – no, a place right here – for both of you.

Dear *Nowhere Special*,

And the 'Dear' is truly meant, deeply felt.

I knew practically nothing about you going into the cinema – and have to say by the time the final credits came up I was sad that I was the only one there. You are the kind of film that many audiences would very much like to see. You are a small film – but that does not mean slight.

While your title is *Nowhere Special*, your particular Nowhere is Northern Ireland, Belfast, the very important somewhere for John and his little boy, Michael. John is a working-class man, a window cleaner (and you do show us quite a lot of suds, swipes, and sparklingly clean windows!), but the Russian mother of his three-year-old son has disappeared back to Russia. John is doing his best to care for Michael, bringing him up well.

I was very impressed with the screen presence and performance by James Norton – quite a long way from his Anglican priest-sleuth in the 1950s village of *Grantchester*, an entertaining television series which I watched through. And the little boy, Daniel Lamont, how could the director get such a realistic performance? I looked up the IMDb to see if James Norton had any children. He doesn't. But I found an article that described how the actor spent a lot of time before and during the making of the film with Daniel and his actual family (who, I notice, are accredited as chaperones during the final credits). Which means that the two obviously got on very well, the little boy comfortable in James Norton's presence. Which also means, I suppose, that all the director had to do was just to ask the little boy to imagine the scene, give him some words, and simply train the camera on him. And that works wonders in terms of his performance. In fact, director, Uberto Pasolini, described Daniel as 'extraordinarily aware and sensitive'.

I want to say that I felt great empathy for John and the little boy – relating to my own experiences. For my brother and myself, our mother died when we were young, leaving our father, age 36, a widower. In this film, John has a birthday cake with 34 candles – and the little boy holding up an ominous extra candle. The theme is how does a father take care of his motherless son. I felt an extraordinary empathy for John.

And then came the complication – that John had a brain tumour, had a limited time to live. And then I realised that he had meetings with social services, that a trainee was accompanying him on various interview visits, that he was looking for a family to whom he could entrust Michael: meeting the different families, listening to them, testing them, their points of view about family, upbringing, love and care, education. Which meant then that we were identifying with John, testing out our own reactions to the different parents, some wealthy, some with a number of children, some very lonely, some uppity, a single mother who had given her child up for adoption.

John does his best but is highly emotional himself, looking at Michael and his responses to the various families, but how can we really read the reactions of a three-year-old?

As I watched James Norton's performance, trying to gauge his character, I found I was thinking back to my interest in personality typology, the work of Carl Jung and the Americans, Katherine Briggs and Isabel Myers. How was John reacting? How did he cope? What are the effects of pressures on him? I realised that he was a quiet type, introverted in his way, relying on himself and his own inner life and in the drives to deal with his illness and finding a home for Michael. As a window cleaner, competent in his work, handy with these details of daily life, he was a focused sensing man. And, again on the personal level, he was moved very much by people and situations, taking his time in making up his mind. Which meant that I was thinking, according to the popular letters, ISFP, and, remembering that according to the theory, this particular profile, neither right or wrong, neither good or bad, could be described as the least assertive profile. I realised that while his death was imminent, John was in no hurry, no rush to settle Michael's adoption until he was satisfied.

By the end of the film, and the delight of a visit to the fair, we have become very familiar with this particular Nowhere Special, the way of life, the daily details, the range of families we have met. And, when John finally makes a decision, I realised I had gone with the flow and fully expected the choice that he actually made.

With no one in the cinema, I could get my handkerchief to my teary eyes without any self-conscious embarrassment.

Dear *The Drover's Wife The Legend of Molly Johnson*,

I remembered that Henry Lawson's 1892 short story is an Australian classic. Then I read that writer/director/actor Leah Purcell has spoken of her love for the story from her childhood, opening up her imagination. But, In later years, she has certainly opened up her imagination in exploring the characters of Lawson's story, shaping the story into a theatre drama, award-winning, then a novel, award-winning. Now she has made you, the film version, an obvious nominee for film awards.

Leah Purcell has made you a darker and bleaker story than Henry Lawson's. She gives a name to your drover's wife, Molly Johnson, her husband seen droving sheep in Snowy Mountain vistas, frequently absent, her living with her children, pregnant as you open. She lives a hard life, surviving, a harsh birth sequence, grief.

You take the audience into Molly Johnson's life, the basic poverty of her hut, and she is seen often busily sweeping to neatness the dusty entry, all austere but surrounded by extraordinary photography of the Snowy Mountains, the landscapes around Adaminaby – although this is the opposite mood from *The Man from Snowy River*.

Meanwhile, you show a local town growing, still somewhat primitive, a young British policeman and his wife pass by the hut, a sympathy for Molly, the wife, eager to write articles on the situation of women in the bush, also eager to help Molly and the children. Some civilised culture is possible in the pioneering town. But her husband is very strictly law and order. And there is a lot to be concerned about: the rough life, the visiting drovers and wanderers, the women and the brothels, the difficulties of imposing order. And there are strict people in the town, Bruce Spence as the local priest, Maggie Dence his austere sister – and some of their taints of racial prejudice and superiority, all delivered with righteous certainty.

However, at the centre of your tale is an Aboriginal man, Yadaka, played by the versatile Rob Collins. He is wanted for murder, turns up at the drover's hut, threatened by Molly, eventually some understanding, appreciating his decency, his helping Molly's oldest son, moments of initiation rituals. He is able to tell his story, a strange story of his being taken from his family, working in a circus, searching for a peaceful place in the bush. This place is a dream of hope in your bleak storytelling. He also has stories about Molly's mother and father which heighten the racial tensions.

And then you become grimmer. The drover's friends turning up, threatening Yadaka, Molly fearing danger for her children, but her then becoming target of the law abiding policeman. You are able to stir deeply as well as stir up all kinds of emotions in us, a greater awareness of Molly's life and pain – and Leah Purcell does not spare us the vicious and raping attack on her, her violent response.

Lawson highlighted the loneliness of the drover's wife, the isolation. This is certainly to the fore in Leah Purcell's interpretation, strengthened by her own powerful screen presence. But she is a force to be reckoned with even as she is victimised – and this interpretation is a fierce indictment of macho arrogance of the 19th century male (and all who are descended from these 19th-century migrants will be alarmed at these aspects of their heritage. My father's side of the family, Malones and Madigans, lived not all that far further north on the southern New South Wales goldfields – forty-two pubs in Araluen alone, my great grandfather's one of them. It is said he forbade drunkenness, swearing and a man had to have his wife's signature on the cheque. How did he make a living?!)

Which means that many of your audiences will see this as a late 19th century, early 20th century #MeToo stand for women and their rights, condemnation of male violence and brutality. This is made especially strong in your final sequences as Molly is hanged, perhaps dramatically unnecessary – or too explicit, the women with their protest aprons defying the men, but nevertheless, thematically relevant, then and now.

Leah Purcell has made of you a drama, bringing her first nation experiences and sensibilities to her writing and to her performance. You are one of those Australian films, along with *The Nightingale*, that, however emotionally tough it might be, should be seen.

Dear *Foul Play*,

I wanted to include you are amongst these letters because you are one of my favourite comedies. I spent two happy months at the end of 1978 studying in Berkeley, frequent visits into San Francisco. However, I just checked and found that you were released in July 78 and so out of the cinemas by the time I arrived.

But this does give me the opportunity to tell you where I did see you. Of all places, in Jerusalem. Taking in all the sights of Jerusalem meant that in the evenings, a visit to local cinemas! Not just a casual outing, security checks in the cinema after each session as we waited in line outside, security checks on each of us before going in. I don't know how that added to the mood, certainties and uncertainties in Israel, but whatever the prologue to seeing you, I did enjoy the experience and have repeated it (not in Jerusalem!) But just recently, in the quietness of my room.

In those days my reviews for *Annals* were limited to about 100 words. I thought you might like to see what I wrote in early 1979:

Foul Play: recommending comedies with so much variation in audience taste is always a risk; but I'll risk it recommended, especially if you're feeling off colour and need some diverting cheering up. How about an assassination attempt on Pope Pius XIII, during a San Francisco gala performance of *The Mikado*? How about car chases, near-miss murders, some screams, Burgess Meredith and Rachel Roberts in a karate fight, plenty of verbal and visual wit? How about Goldie Hawn at her most attractive and in the middle of the foul play and romance with comedian Chevy Chase? How about Dudley Moore in one of his best sketches? Writer, (Silver Streak)-director Colin Higgins has it all there delightfully.

I just noticed the reference to *Silver Streak* and realise that this was 1979 and Colin Higgins had great success in 1980 with *Nine-to-Five*. (I always had a soft spot for Colin Higgins when I heard that he had spent some years at the Franciscan junior at school in Robertson, on the New South Wales southern Highlands, when my uncle was teaching there in the early 1950s. He must've had his tongue firmly in cheek inventing the Catholic themes for you here.)

I am going to enjoy myself, some happy déjà vu, in listing what I so much enjoyed in watching you.

First of all, I do enjoy a comedy-thriller, all kinds of murders, bodies disappearing, and quite a rogues' gallery of villains. And, who could resist a San Francisco setting, glimpses of the city, and, of course, the mad taxi chase, the elderly Japanese tourists enjoying it all, up and down the San Francisco Hills, outbulleting Bullitt, and back again for *What's up Doc*. Seeing you after spending the two months there, was a delight, but watching you again decades later, a wonderful reminder.

And, it was the 1970s, *Saturday Night Fever* (and Dudley Moore's strip), Barry Manilow – but, of course, the scenes from *The Mikado*, Pope Pius XIII thoroughly enjoying it, the homage to Hitchcock's *The Man Who Knew Too Much* and the assassination attempt during the performance, and the courteous but rather oblivious-to-danger-Pope leading the applause.

And, I did enjoy the Catholic themes. After all, John Paul II was elected while I was in Berkeley. The film anticipated him and his love of music and concerts and acting. And who can resist the initial assassination of an Archbishop! And his fraudster twin brother and his evil mentor, Rachel Roberts as Miss Caswall.

There was plenty to enjoy in the verbal humour – especially filling in the blanks in the elderly ladies' Scrabble game! And, of course, plenty of visual humour. There was the mixup with the Dwarf, and the poor actual dwarf arriving with his sales spiel, Goldie Hawn fighting him, his falling out the window, hospital, her visiting him – and his dread as he was strung up there with her intention to bat off the fly on his chest. But the real Dwarf, was the albino, frightening Goldie Hawn in the library.

And veteran Burgess Meredith as Mr Hennessey, the landlord, his snake, Esme, and the martial arts fight with Miss Caswall.

Well, Goldie Hawn was a favourite at that time and Chevy Chase emerging as a popular comedian, there was also Dudley Moore, turning up at the singles bar, at the sex shop, at the massage parlour, and the delightful final irony that there he was, the conductor of *The Mikado*.

Just glancing back over that list, it is quite an amount of comedy. I wonder did Colin Higgins sit in his room and make a list of all the funny aspects he could think of, the thriller aspects... Whether he did or not, he was eminently successful. I think I'll try to watch you again!

Dear *Good Luck to you, Leo Grande*,

Well, there I was, sitting at the cinema at the Jam Factory, knowing in general what you are about but conscious of having to write for a Catholic readership. On the subject, sex and sexuality. And, your reviewer, a long-time celibate priest. Not exactly the challenge for others at the preview audience. So, I'm taking something of an easy way out – not entirely – and sending you the review that I wrote. Here it is:

> A sex worker is hired by a widowed religious education teacher for an evening at a hotel.
>
> That answers the question: *what* is the film about? It does not indicate *how* the subject is treated, though there is a genial message in the title for Leo Grande, the sex worker.
>
> The film is a two-hander which could be performed on stage. It consists mainly of dialogue and is expertly performed by Emma Thompson as Nancy and Daryl McCormack as Leo, Irish and with his accent.
>
> Watching Leo and Nancy at the press preview made me realise that there were two basic responses. For 'secular' Western audiences, the film was an interesting, often humorous, easy watch, comfortable in talking about bodies, male and female, about sexual experience and pleasure, about looking at past attitudes and restraints, restrictions, about new calmer freedoms. This is a particularly Western society perspective.
>
> But there is another approach to a film dealing with sexuality, perhaps a subject that is too private and delicate for a film dramatisation. And the question arises as to what we mean by prudish and how much of this is sensitivity,

how much fear of the subject. Many cultures and many religions and church traditions approach from a more prescriptive perspective: Thou shalt, Thou shalt not... (With an intransigent intolerance).

In the film, Leo Grande represents the former view. He is more than comfortable in his chosen role as a sex worker, providing a service, perhaps able to provide some healing for a client's bad past experiences or attitudes (except that he has not told his mother). That is his philosophy of life and he is at ease with it.

Nancy, on the other hand, is very straight-up-and-down in all aspects of her life, with her husband of three decades, her children (though she finds her son boring, her daughter reckless). And she has been strict with the girls in school, especially in essays on sexual morality. She likes plans, order, lists... But in her late 50s, she realises she feels deprived, her sexual life having been one of very matter-of-fact, brief and rapid 'conjugal duties'. No corresponding awareness, of course, of sexual pleasure. (Memories of Robert Mitchum and Sarah Miles, fifty years ago, dramatising the matter-of-fact proper conjugal rights and duties and *Ryan's Daughter* dissatisfied, yearnings, set in an Irish Catholic moral framework of commandments and expectations.)

Now, two years a widow, Nancy has hired Leo, a list of suggestions of what is to be done.

Yes, there is sexual activity. However, it is in the context of four meetings between Nancy and Leo, their discussions, telling their stories (and sometimes not), analysing past codes and their inadequacies, speculating on changing attitudes and behaviour, Nancy and a sexual curiosity, a desire for awakening late in life.

Leo faces some of his own realities, challenged by Nancy. Nancy is very much challenged, has a revealing confession conversation with a past pupil and, eventually, stands at the mirror, naked, acknowledging the reality and limits of her body.

Which means that the audience realises, at the end, they have been looking at the film as in a mirror, looking at bodies, sexual activity, pleasure, mirror-testing their own values and stances, wondering about their own reflections. In the past sixty years, Catholic theological reflection on sexuality has moved from Moral Theology Manuals and their declarations of principles to a deeper understanding of marriage, psychological awareness and even, as with Pope John Paul II and his writings, a theology of the body.

And we remember that this is just a film, just over ninety minutes, two characters, conversations, personal and moral questions, particular perspectives – and remembering that it does not cover every aspect of sexuality and relationships, that they can be helpful conversations (as Leo and Nancy find out). For instance, the renewed Catholic moral awareness of deeper aspects of sexuality and marriage could provide further questions in challenges.

And there is always the answer to the Gospel question: how did Jesus relate to sex workers?

Dear *The Bombardment*,

I still find it surprising that each year, surprising in many ways since it is eighty years plus and minus since the harrowing events of World War II, there are so many films dramatising aspects of that war.

You might think that we have seen so many that there is no need for more. And the films have taken us to Germany itself, to the Nazi invasions of the continent and the occupations, Battle of Britain, entry of the US into the war, the bombing of Pearl Harbor, the Japanese and war in the Pacific. Is there a need for so many war films?

And the answer is, of course: Lest we forget.

With your drama, based on a true story (very sadly), you take us to Denmark, the city of Copenhagen, March 1945, almost at the end of the war. Your screenplay is clever, intricate, introducing us to five strands in the story which eventually and tragically come together. You set your tone vividly in the opening, three young women happily getting dressed, off to a marriage ceremony, a benign old taxi driver, jollity – and then a plane swooping out of the sky and strafing the car killing them all. And the witness is a young boy, Henry, riding his bike, delivering cartons of eggs. He is overwhelmed by what he sees, traumatised, from then on unable to speak. And we are overwhelmed with him.

The strafing is by the RAF, revealed to be mistaken identity, the consequences weighing heavily on the pilots. Isn't that a dreadful phrase, that there is death from 'friendly fire'?

I have just re-read a paragraph from my review of you. I mentioned the five strands of plot and have just added the role of the RAF, but now I see that I was rather overwhelmed by how much you introduce, such different characters, Nazi sympathisers and the anti-Nazi Resistance. The killing in the street and the little girls and their mothers watching. And you took me completely by surprise in introducing the character of the penitential nun.

I thought I would let you see the paragraph: 'We are also introduced to a young man, condemned by his father, discovering that he is working for the occupying Germans. Then one of his friends is confronted in the street by a resistance member. He is shot, and witnessed by mothers and little girls. It emerges that the little girls go to a French school in Copenhagen, that Henry is a cousin of one of them and he goes to the school, managed by a community of sisters. The focus is on one of the sisters, Teresa, penitential, flogging herself, questioning God's presence and absence, criticised by the superior community, yet devoted to the girls. She has also encountered the German collaborator and told him that he is the devil. But, there is a strange attraction between them.'

By now your plot is ready for the central action. I don't think that we, the audience, really are ready. It requires some stores of emotional strength to continue watching. The Germans are occupying a large building in central Copenhagen, the Shell House, and the Resistance are requesting the RAF to bomb it, even if some of their members are in cells immediately under the roof. We see the preparations, the planning by the RAF, three squads, setting out for the bombing, the first reaching its target.

However, your harrowing drama of the bombardment is the mistaking by two of the squads for the French school as Shell House. From then on, your drama is vivid, highly dramatic, tragic, the bombs and fires, the nuns and children killed and injured, hurrying to the basement, trapped, the attempted rescue... With such suffering of the innocent children, you become even harder to watch. As is the aftermath, the anxious parents, the nun and one of the little girls beneath the building, water rising, and Henry, dismayed, but finding a task of identifying girls being taken to hospital, writing notes, taking them to the theatre for an actress to read out the details to anguishing parents.

This is not a spoiler, but your ending, narrowly focused, is not what we were quite expecting at all, but gives us a moment of relief before the final credits come up and there is a listing of all those who are killed, especially the names of the children, so many of them.

Yes, it is difficult to watch you, but you are recommended.

Dear *Maxaibel, The Best of Enemies, Mass*,

I am taking some liberties in writing to the three of you rather than to one movie. But I wanted to complete this book with a very serious tone.

In fact, the letter was intended for four movies but a key film, not seen yet, is not yet available on streaming as promised. It is the 2017 film, directed by Roland Joffe (*The Killing Fields, The Mission*), *The Forgiven*, a story of The Truth and Reconciliation Commission of post-apartheid South Africa with Forest Whitaker as Archbishop Desmond Tutu. You will realise where this is leading. I wanted to write to four movies that I've watched this year, each dramatising the significance of truth and reconciliation, restorative justice, healing.

Since the 1990s, I have been impressed and amazed at what has happened in South Africa – offering the world a significant model for healing, in the vein of St Francis' Peace Prayer. And I have wondered why the model was not taken up by the Catholic Church, by other churches and organisations, in contributing to the healing of sexual abuse cases, meetings between survivors and abuses (I know this has happened at times) but the emphasis has been on litigation and compensation, necessary though they may be.

But I want to let each of you know the truth and reconciliation impact you made.

At the press preview of the Spanish Film Festival this year, we were shown you, *Maxaibel*. Your central character had every reason not to forgive – criminal murder of her husband, grief, hardening of heart. I was intrigued by your setting, having been aware of the actions, motivation, violence of Basque Separatists,

ETA. But, somehow rather, I had missed this reconciliation movement of the 2000s, of the significance of long-time political activist, Maxaibel, her interviews with one of the convicted killers, achieving something akin to what had happened in South Africa – despite decades of hostilities, violence and brutality, peace is possible.

Then I came across you, *Best of Enemies*, on Netflix. I had never heard of you though you are from 2019. More's the pity. The word your screenplay uses for meetings of hostile, ideologically opposing individuals and groups, was a word that I was unfamiliar with, charrette. I was pleased to discover what it meant. To save any Googling: charrette is a public meeting or workshop devoted to a concerted effort to solve a problem or plan the design of something.

I should say I was particular interested in your context – 1971, Durham, North Carolina, Martin Luther King and Civil Rights development and integration advances, school segregation predominating. You also show the Ku Klux Klan. Sam Rockwell plays C.P.Ellis, a garage technician, local head of the Klan, who had grown up in bigotry. His enemy is black organiser, Ann Atwater, Taraji P. Henson at her most demandingly vigorous. But a judge imposes a charrette on Durham and these two are the chairs of their respective groups and respective stances. Not easy. Enmity, but having to sit next to each other at meals, black next to white.

You are a true story, taking us through the enmity, some crumbling of barriers, some humanity beside redneck inflexibility. And we learn that these enemies worked together for years afterwards, speaking out for justice.

Then it was you, *Mass*. You were on the list of nominations for awards from the US-based International Association of Catholic Critics. In Australia, we had never heard of you. Then, suddenly, you were programmed for the International Melbourne Film Festival. Then I could see the reasons for the nominations.

I had to get through to understand your title, *Mass*, with, for me, Catholic redemptive tones, forgiveness and atonement. Then it was pointed out, 'Mass' murder. Your story is of that all too frequent American occurrence – school, students and teachers, gun massacres.

Your focus is quite confined but making the drama and intense dialogue (without any visual flashbacks) all the more powerful and disturbing. And, the setting for the meeting is a room adjacent to a church.

You make us spend time (and emotions) as the parents of the dead boys sit with the parents of the student shooter. Truth and Reconciliation is not achieved instantly and has been in progress before this meeting. The four parents have permission to vent their distress and grief, loss of their sons, the mystery of being the parents of the disturbed shooter being blamed by association. A tribute to you and your writer and director (Fran Kranz) and your cast, each with their dramatic outbursts, their quiet moments, the clash between mind and heart, and the final sentiment in so many of these stories: 'I can't forgive yet. Give me some time and I will try'.

So it looks like a hearty vote of thanks to the three of you – national reconciliation, local truth, families and forgiveness and peace.

I continue to be on the lookout for *The Forgiven*, my next Dear Movie.

TITLES IN ALPHABETICAL ORDER

Ad Astra
All That Jazz
Belle Epoque, La
Best Of Enemies
Black Narcissus
Blue Bayou
Bombardment, The
Crocodile Dundee
Curtain: Poirot's Last Case
Dead Man Walking
Devil All The Time, The
Departures/Okuributo
Drover's Wife The Legend Of Molly Johnson, The
Duel
Empire Strikes Back, The
Enola Holmes
Erin Brockovich
Fantasia
Fargo
Father, The
For The Boys
Foul Play
Free Guy
Glory
Good Catholic, The

Good Luck To You, Leo Grande
Good, The Bad And The Ugly, The
Great Expectations/Oliver Twist
Gunman's Walk
Hail, Caesar
Hereafter
Hope Gap
Incendies
Innocentes, Les
Irving Berlin: An American Song
I Still See You
It Must Be Heaven
Inception
Insult, The/ L'insulte
Jo Jo Rabbit
Joker
Judy And Punch
Kingdom Of Heaven
Last Full Measure, The
Last Temptation Of Christ, The
Life And Death Of Colonel Blimp, The
Maxaibel
Mary And Max
Mass
Mass Appeal
Matter Of Life And Death, A
Monsieur Vincent
Mosul
Mrs Lowry And Son

Murder Most Foul
Name Of The Rose, The
Nightingale, The
Nomadland
Nowhere Special
One Second
Ophelia
Path To War
Pawnbroker, The
Phone Booth
Professor And His Beloved Equation
Quo Vadis
Rabbit-proof Fence
Raiders Of The Lost Ark
Rainmaker, The
Remember
Report, The
Riders Of Justice
Score To Settle, A
Scott Of The Antarctic
Second Civil War, The
Se7en
Shutter Island
Six Degrees Of Separation
Some Like It Hot
Sorry We Missed You
Star Is Born, A
To Sir With Love
Tootsie

Tree Of Life, The
West Side Story/West Side Story
Winter Light
Words On A Bathroom Wall
Worth

www.ingramcontent.com/pod-product-compliance
Lightning Source LLC
Chambersburg PA
CBHW012003090526
44590CB00026B/3858